HBR Guide to **Crafting Your Purpose**

Harvard Business Review Guides

Arm yourself with the advice you need to succeed on the job, from the most trusted brand in business. Packed with how-to essentials from leading experts, the HBR Guides provide smart answers to your most pressing work challenges.

The titles include:

HBR Guide for Women at Work
HBR Guide to Being More Productive
HBR Guide to Better Business Writing
HBR Guide to Building Your Business Case
HBR Guide to Buying a Small Business
HBR Guide to Changing Your Career
HBR Guide to Coaching Employees
HBR Guide to Collaborative Teams
HBR Guide to Data Analytics Basics for Managers
HBR Guide to Dealing with Conflict
HBR Guide to Delivering Effective Feedback
HBR Guide to Emotional Intelligence
HBR Guide to Finance Basics for Managers
HBR Guide to Getting the Mentoring You Need
HBR Guide to Getting the Right Job
HBR Guide to Getting the Right Work Done
HBR Guide to Leading Teams
HBR Guide to Making Better Decisions
HBR Guide to Making Every Meeting Matter

HBR Guide to Managing Strategic Initiatives

HBR Guide to Managing Stress at Work

HBR Guide to Managing Up and Across

HBR Guide to Motivating People

HBR Guide to Negotiating

HBR Guide to Networking

HBR Guide to Office Politics

HBR Guide to Performance Management

HBR Guide to Persuasive Presentations

HBR Guide to Project Management

HBR Guide to Remote Work

HBR Guide to Setting Your Strategy

HBR Guide to Thinking Strategically

HBR Guide to Work-Life Balance

HBR Guide to Your Professional Growth

HBR Guide to **Crafting Your Purpose**

John Coleman

HARVARD BUSINESS REVIEW PRESS

Boston, Massachusetts

Printed in the United States of America
10 9 8 7 6 5 4 3 2 1

Library of Congress Cataloging-in-Publication Data

Names: Coleman, John, 1981– author.
Title: HBR guide to crafting your purpose / John Coleman.
Other titles: Harvard Business Review guide to crafting your purpose | Harvard business review guides.
Description: Boston, Massachusetts : Harvard Business Review Press, [2022] | Series: HBR guides | Includes index.
Identifiers: LCCN 2021034693 (print) | LCCN 2021034694 (ebook) | ISBN 9781633699830 (paperback) | ISBN 9781633699847 (ebook)
Subjects: LCSH: Job enrichment. | Quality of work life. | Self-actualization (Psychology)
Classification: LCC HF5549.5.J616 C63 2022 (print) | LCC HF5549.5.J616 (ebook) | DDC 658.3/1423--dc23
LC record available at https://lccn.loc.gov/2021034693
LC ebook record available at https://lccn.loc.gov/2021034694
ISBN: 978-1-63369-983-0
eISBN: 978-1-63369-984-7

The paper used in this publication meets the requirements of the American National Standard for Permanence of Paper for Publications and Documents in Libraries and Archives Z39.48-1992.

What You'll Learn

Do you struggle to find purpose in your professional or personal life? You're not alone. We have all heard stories where someone suddenly discovers their life's purpose out of the blue—that *one* thing that gives their lives meaning. But most of us will not magically stumble upon a single purpose that makes everything we do worthwhile. Instead, we need to proactively craft and shape multiple purposes over the course of our lives and careers.

Whether you are new to the workforce, in the middle of your career, or facing a career transition, this guide will provide you with tips and advice for mining all areas of your life for purpose. Through stories of real people, from bus drivers to executives, you'll see how you can then take what you've found and shape it into a life of meaning—without requiring you to leave your job.

You'll learn how to:

- Dispel three common myths about purpose
- Confront and address feelings of monotony in your life

- Cultivate your interests and hobbies to better find purpose
- Invest in multiple sources of meaning, including love, beauty, and service
- Let go of past purposes and overcome your aversion to change
- Use job crafting to shape your role into the job you want
- Identify opportunities for craft and task mastery in your work
- Develop positive relationships—both personally and professionally
- Connect what you do to serving others
- Create a culture of purpose in your team and organization
- Live into corporate purpose and ensure that it sticks

Contents

Introduction

Curtis Jenkins is a marvel. On May 24, 2019, CBS Evening News aired a short segment about the school bus driver from Dallas who must be among the most purposeful men in America. I spent two years on a public school board in Georgia, and I know that driving a school bus—while remarkably important—can be grueling and thankless. But Curtis approaches his work with energy, optimism, skill, and care.

Curtis doesn't simply drive the bus; he creates what the segment referred to as a "yellow bus utopia." He assigns each of the children responsibilities on the bus—police officers, administrative assistants—and he turns each journey into an exercise in community. His technical job is simply to pick kids up at their bus stops, drop them at Lake Highlands Elementary, and return them safely in the afternoon. But he's crafted his work into so much more.

"These are my children," he says in the segment. "These are my community. I love 'em all."

And what's striking beyond Curtis's creativity is the deep joy he so clearly takes in his work—his eyes dance, his smile is infectious—and the extraordinary care he invests in his passengers. His kids' comments say it all:

"He really cares about us."

"He's really kind."

"[H]e helps anyone in need."

"He's the father that I always wanted."

As the producers of the clip note, "We make the mistake sometimes of thinking certain jobs are more important than others. But Curtis Jenkins *made* his job important."

He takes the ordinary and makes it extraordinary.

A Life of Purpose

Do you feel as essential and empowered as Curtis Jenkins?

Do you have his sense of wonder and passion for work and a commitment to engaging everything you do with excellence?

Do you live daily with a sense of purpose and significance?

I've spent the last 25 years working with every type of organization and person. I was a busboy at Applebee's and a sales associate at an outdoor sports and fitness chain. I have spent time as a writing tutor, a think tank intern, an energy trader, and a management consultant. And I've glimpsed inside nonprofits, government entities, and businesses large and small. I've been privileged to work or go to school with doctors, NGO founders, entrepreneurs, teachers, investment bankers, priests, and almost everything in between.

Through all those experiences, I've learned there is little correlation between the type of work a person does and how meaningful or purposeful their life feels. I've met teachers who deeply felt the high calling of their profession—caring for and instructing kids, offering them an equal opportunity at life through education—and I've met teachers who felt hopeless and abandoned. I've met incredibly wealthy, successful men and women who couldn't think of a reason to live. And I've encountered fast-food workers who were so filled with joy that they turned around my day in a moment's interaction. I've met demotivated, angry people in world-changing NGOs and driven, altruistic people in large for-profit corporations.

I bet you have, too.

All these contradictions lead me to believe that most of us labor under false assumptions about purpose. Correcting those assumptions is critical to creating meaning and significance in our lives. Purpose isn't a pot of gold at the end of the rainbow, something mystical you stumble into that gives your life meaning. It's at once both simpler and more complex than that.

Ten years ago, I published a book about next-generation leadership called *Passion and Purpose*. On the heels of the great financial crisis, that book was intended to explore key themes that would shape leadership over the next several decades through the prisms of both data and individual stories. A recurring theme my coauthors and I encountered was the desire for purpose and significance. We found that the desire for purpose trumped almost everything else in a person's professional pursuits.

We all need purpose in our life. Research and common sense tell us that purpose is essential to a "good" or flourishing life. And yet many of us feel a lack of purpose in our lives and especially in our work.

We don't have to live that way. Purpose isn't magic—it's something we must consciously pursue and create. With the right approach, almost any job—any life—can be meaningful.

Building Your Individual Purpose

What's your story? Maybe there's something missing from your job or life and you're not sure exactly what it is. Your life may be good, but you feel it lacks significance and deeper meaning. You've taken sensible or necessary roles, but you've never really felt them to be meaningful or motivating. Or perhaps you once had a sense of purpose but have lost it as you've fallen into the rhythm of a typical adult life—with a mortgage, a bevy of bills, and an ever-increasing sense of responsibility. Perhaps you work in a field that you believe should be incredibly purposeful—medicine, teaching, or foundation work, for example—but after years of monotony or disappointment you now struggle to make your work meaningful on a day-to-day basis. Maybe you're just starting out and want to find a path in life that you feel is worth pursuing.

If so, this book is for you. In the 10 years since I wrote *Passion and Purpose*, I've had a lot of time to think about the topic of purpose. I've heard endless questions about it in audiences to which I've spoken. I've seen written comments about it on my articles. I've had friends ask me about it. And I've struggled with it in my life and work—often feeling my own career was meaningless and my own life wasted.

And in all that reflection and struggle, I've come to believe that our current crisis of meaning stems from a particularly destructive modern conception of the term "purpose," the ways we "find" it, and the role it plays in our lives. This conception rests on a series of myths that can be revealed, understood, and corrected. And once we correct these myths we can learn to uncover, build, and craft the different sources of meaning in each of our lives.

You don't have to leave your job (though you may choose to do so). You don't have to radically change your life (though you can if you need to). But you will have to think differently about the way you live and work and the meaning you make in everything that you do.

The most inspiring people we encounter—people like Curtis—aren't inspiring by accident. They don't find their purpose, they build it. Their stories aren't accidents, they are authored.

If you're sick of looking for your purpose, I hope that with the help of this book you can stop searching and start building.

What This Book Will Do

This book aims to help you craft a life and a career filled with purpose. Whether you are new to the workforce, further along in your career, or somewhere in between, this guide is filled with tips and advice for building meaning and purpose into everything you do—without requiring you to uproot your life or work. It's meant to be used in whatever way works best for your needs. You can sit down one Sunday afternoon and read it cover-to-cover with a cup of coffee or drop in occasionally reading relevant chapters in 5–10-minute chunks.

The book has four primary sections:

Section 1: Getting Started with Purpose. We all need purpose. But what is it? Why is it so essential to a balanced life, and why does its absence cause so many problems? We'll take a moment here to define purpose and explore the problems that arise from a lack of purpose in people's lives at both the individual and societal level. Then, I provide an exercise for you to reflect on where you currently find meaning in your life as a starting point for the rest of your purpose journey.

Section 2: Redefining How We Think About Purpose. We then dive into the three myths most people hold about purpose: that purpose is a thing you find, that it's a single thing, and that it's static over time. We'll explore instead how purpose is mined and made, how it is plural, and how it changes—introducing exercises that will help you to better see and develop the sources of meaning in your life.

Section 3: Building Your Purpose. This section explores, more deeply, the topic of purpose at work—helping you to craft your work, make work a craft, connect your work to service, and invest in positive relationships. The frameworks and exercises in this section are designed to help you zero in on how to make your professional life more meaningful.

Section 4: Purpose in Your Organization. While sections 1–3 primarily focus on how we, as individuals, can craft purpose in our own lives, section 4 focuses on what a culture of corporate purpose looks like and how to create it. Whether you're currently a senior leader in your organization or simply aspire to be, you'll learn a multitude of ways people at all levels can impact corporate purpose.

Throughout the book, I have embedded frameworks and exercises for you to complete while reading. These exercises will help you reflect on purpose and formulate concrete plans to craft more meaning in your life. The goal, by the end, is to help you not only think differently about purpose but to have a strategy in hand for a more purposeful life.

SECTION ONE

Getting Started with Purpose

CHAPTER 1

Purpose, and Why It Matters

What is purpose? Put simply, purpose is what gives your work and life meaning and importance—a sense of impact, depth, and direction. It's a concept most of us understand intuitively. But why does it matter? Because its absence can be devastating and its presence is essential to flourishing. And many people currently struggle with the sometimes-catastrophic consequences of a perceived lack of meaning in their lives.

In 2012, Chris Arnade was an affluent, accomplished trader at a premier New York bank. In purely material terms, he'd been wildly successful and lived a classic version of the American dream. Born in a small town in Florida to middle-class parents (a professor and a librarian), Chris went on to college, a PhD program at Johns Hopkins, and a trading desk in New York City. He had wealth, a nice apartment, and kids in private school—yet he grew weary of the job and the life that had provided him with this success.

So, Chris, who liked to walk and explore New York on foot, began photographing some of the city's poorest areas—notably Hunt's Point—spending time with local residents who became his friends. As his photography hobby began to overwhelm his desire to work his day job, Chris left his Wall Street bank and turned to writing and photography full time.

He still struggled. He went through a period of drug and alcohol abuse. And as he explored the poorest parts of New York—and then of America, visiting often-overlooked towns in Alabama, Ohio, and dozens of states in between—he began to document, in his writing and photography, parts of America in quiet crisis. Terming these places and the people in them "back row" America, Chris documented hundreds of people striving for meaning, dignity, survival, and love even while struggling with substance abuse, homelessness, poverty, and despair. His book, *Dignity*, documents this journey and the people he came to know along the way. His own struggles for purpose and significance demonstrate things aren't entirely well in "front row" America either.

Chris's book isn't the first or last to focus on the desperate search for meaning, dignity, respect, and belonging in modern America. The anecdotes are nearly endless—articles, novels, nonfiction books, and screenplays—a collective voice testifying to an era in which people are struggling to find happiness, meaning, significance, belonging, and yes, purpose. And, of course, almost all of us experience or see less dramatic and less public versions of these stories every day:

- The accountant who lives well but struggles to connect her 40 hours per week to the higher calling she's always longed for
- The teacher who sacrificed to get into a profession where he could change lives but has become bogged down and cynical about his work
- The CEO who's found success and wealth but feels empty
- The journalist who's found fame but doesn't feel her work is driving real change
- The police officer who feels overwhelmed by the social problems he confronts each shift
- The stay-at-home mom who feels so overwhelmed by the minute-by-minute challenges of her kids that she's lost sight of the joys of parenting

Day in and day out superficially well-off people are burning out and struggling to see the deeper meaning in their lives and work. For some, this is merely a matter of turning a good life into a great life. For others, however, it's a matter of urgency—a crisis. The good news is that if you are feeling this way, you are far from alone.

A Crisis of Meaning

Before the Covid-19 pandemic upended life around the world, we were living in the most prosperous period in all of human history, and yet people weren't happier or more fulfilled. Why? A rising collection of data confirm and illuminate the disconnect between prosperity and purpose.

An incredibly high number of people express dissatisfaction with their jobs. A recent study sought to more accurately define the term "good job" and determine how many Americans had them. The survey found the top three components of a "good job" were enjoyable day-to-day work, stable and predictable pay, and a sense of purpose—but also found only 40% of employees felt they had these things.[1] Mental Health America recently released a survey on workplace satisfaction that found 81% of respondents felt their work stress created family problems, 63% said work stress caused them to engage in unhealthy behaviors, 71% spent time speaking badly about their company or boss, and 71% spent time each week thinking about or looking for a new job.[2] And a recent Gallup survey found that while the number of employees who feel "engaged" at work is the highest it's been in years, that number is still only 34% in the United States and 15% internationally.[3] A prior survey found that only 27% of these employees believe in their company's values.[4]

Outside of work, the picture grows grimmer—many people are stressed out and unhappy. The *World Happiness Report*, for example, analyzes three primary measures of happiness, and all three are at or near record lows.[5] The 2019 U.S. General Social Survey reported unhappiness levels higher than at any point since the 2007 financial crisis—and, before that, since the 1970s.[6] And the *2019 Gallup Global Emotions Report* found stress, worry, and anger among people around the world at multi-year highs.[7]

These increases in anger and stress are being accompanied by a surge in loneliness. Harvard professor Robert Putnam first brought widespread attention to social isolation and loneliness—social capital—in the United States in his seminal book *Bowling Alone*. And more recent surveys of social connection and loneliness are not indicative of progress since that time. A 2016 survey, for example, found that 72% of Americans experience loneliness, almost a third on a weekly basis.[8] And a 2018 study by Cigna documented similar results. By their measures, nearly half of Americans feel lonely and 54% say that no one knows them well. Results are particularly acute among younger Americans.[9] And outside the United States similar results have been documented in Canada, for example, with the United Kingdom going so far as to appoint a "minister for loneliness."[10] Numerous countries, seeing these statistics, are taking the problem of loneliness seriously as a public health crisis.

It remains to be seen whether the Covid-19 pandemic and other recent crises change this fundamental dynamic. The disease and associated social and economic fallout have wrought unparalleled devastation—tens of millions ill, millions dead, hundreds of millions who have suffered intense economic hardship, and untold psychological trauma for billions around the world. Indeed, the sheer scale of the pandemic and its impacts could make things dramatically worse. They could also, counterintuitively, reconnect us to things that matter—a small silver lining in the midst of devastation. We likely won't know for some time. And, of course, there are problems globally—racism, inequality, war, and poverty—that have very real negative impacts on peoples' lives and need to be addressed.

But what's certain—what stories like Chris Arnade's and statistics like those above tell us—is that we won't get happier or more fulfilled as the world gets richer and safer. In some ways this social-level data mirrors the various studies recently indicating that there is an ideal income range for well-being somewhere between $65,000 and $105,000 (in the United States—it differs by country) and anything above or below that actually leads to less happiness.[11] Even if the numbers are slightly wrong, we almost all believe the old adage that "money can't buy happiness"; and the data indicate that something is off in the areas we find meaning other than material success.

There's something happening at a social and emotional level that is hollowing out how we experience life, even in places like the United States. And a lot of this looks like a crisis not of simple material circumstances, but of meaning, belonging, trust, and significance. We can have everything, and still want something different.

Conversely, some people can start with very little and end up with an incredibly enriching life. What's their secret?

Where Are You Today?

As you tackle purpose in your own life, it's important to remember that everyone's view of what is meaningful is different. And where you are in crafting your purpose depends on your own personal situation and the context around you.

Take a moment to reflect on where you are right now. Your thoughts on how you're currently feeling about your life and its meaning will be a solid foundation on which to work through the rest of this book. Think of this as a real-time diagnostic of how you're processing purpose today.

1. Do you feel you've ever had a clear sense of purpose?
2. At what point in your past did your life feel most meaningful? Why?
3. How do you feel right now? Why?
4. On a scale of 1–10 (where 10 represents a great deal of purpose and 1 represents no sense of purpose), describe how much purpose you feel in each of the following and why:

    - Your work
    - Your professional relationship
    - Your personal relationships
    - Your service to others

    If you find yourself below an "8" in any area, you have an opportunity for increased meaning in your life.

5. Has there been something in your life this year that's given you a greater sense of meaning? Something that robbed you of meaning?

6. Why are you reading this book, and what do you hope to get from it? Reflect seriously here in two to three paragraphs and return to them periodically while reading. Your observations will offer fruitful areas to focus as you work through the book and exercises.

NOTES

1. Jonathan Rothwell and Steve Crabtree, "Not Just a Job: New Evidence on the Quality of Work in the United States," Gallup, https://www.luminafoundation.org/wp-content/uploads/2019/11/not-just-a-job-new-evidence-on-the-quality-of-work-in-the-united-states.pdf.
2. Faas Foundation, "Mind the Workplace," https://www.mhanational.org/sites/default/files/Mind%20the%20Workplace%20-%20MHA%20Workplace%20Health%20Survey%202017%20FINAL.pdf.
3. Ken Royal, "What Engaged Employees Do Differently," Gallup, September 14, 2019, https://www.gallup.com/workplace/266822/engaged-employees-differently.aspx.
4. Royal, "What Engaged Employees Do Differently."
5. John F. Helliwell, Richard Layard, and Jeffrey Sachs, eds., *World Happiness Report 2019* (New York: Sustainable Development Network, 2019), 15–16.
6. 2019 General Social Survey, NORC at the University of Chicago.
7. *Gallup 2019 Global Emotions Report*, https://www.gallup.com/analytics/248906/gallup-global-emotions-report-2019.aspx.
8. American Osteopathic Association, "Survey Finds Nearly Three-Quarters (72%) of Americans Feel Lonely," PR Newswire, October 11, 2016, https://www.prnewswire.com/news-releases/survey-finds-nearly-three-quarters-72-of-americans-feel-lonely-300342742.html.
9. Aric Jenkins, "Study Finds That Half of Americans—Especially Young People—Feel Lonely," *Fortune*, May 1, 2018, https://fortune.com/2018/05/01/americans-lonely-cigna-study/.
10. LifeWorks, "Loneliness and Isolation Is a Global Problem," January 31, 2019, https://www.lifeworks.com/blog/loneliness-and-isolation-is-a-global-problem/.
11. Jamie Ducharme, "This Is the Amount of Money You Need to Be Happy, According to Research," *Money*, February 14, 2018, http://money.com/money/5157625/ideal-income-study/.

CHAPTER 2

Identifying Your Starting Point

Rufus Massey was born in Chickamauga on the Georgia side of Lookout Mountain and grew up in a rough board, two-room cabin his dad had built by hand. There was no phone service. Getting to school was often challenging, but he managed to make it. "[Y]ou don't know that you have things difficult when you're in that situation," Rufus told me. "So, you make the best of it."

When he'd drive to visit his grandmother in Atlanta, his family would pass Berry College—a beautiful, bucolic campus dotted by old gothic buildings—and he committed to attending one day. Little did he know that Berry was founded in 1902 by one of the twentieth century's most remarkable women, Martha Berry, precisely to serve poor mountain kids like Rufus. He made it in, met his wife on campus, worked all four years, and after a one-year sojourn as a high school biology teacher and wrestling coach after graduation, joined Berry full time in Student Affairs and Student Activities—working on campus for 10 years.

Rufus eventually left for a job at BellSouth and a new opportunity to learn. But after 16 years, the draw of higher education—his initial passport down from Lookout Mountain—was too strong, and Rufus went back to Berry. “I like to see people light up when they learn something new,” Rufus told me. “Educators all think that way. They want to pass along what they know so the next generation can build upon that.”

At Berry he started back in development and moved into alumni relations before the president of the school, Steve Briggs, tapped him for a new program they were considering: Student Enterprises. Part of Martha Berry’s legacy was a well-developed student work program in which most students are expected to hold a part-time job on campus. But Steve and Rufus had a new idea—to turn some of those jobs into real businesses and turn them over completely to students who would serve as owners and leaders rather than just employees. Rufus loved it. “For me it’s back to this purpose thing,” Rufus says, “One of my purposes is to develop leaders.”

Nearly a thousand students went through that program under Rufus. He describes some of them with tears in his eyes while we talked, so proud of what they’d accomplished. Rufus walked into a 100-year-old program and helped craft it into something more meaningful.

He’s led at least three separate careers. He’s mentored hundreds of people. He has a family he’s proud of. He sings in a barbershop quartet and on nationally competitive a cappella teams. He plays tennis with his wife. And he still gets back to his family's cabin on Lookout Mountain to chop firewood and remember the place his life started.

When you speak to Rufus, he listens, he's attentive, he smiles—he seems genuinely interested in you and sincerely happy. In a world experiencing a crisis of meaning, Rufus seems to have it in abundance. In contrast to the lives we explored in chapter 1, Rufus's life seems balanced and flourishing. How does he do it? How can we?

The Secret to Balance and Fulfillment

People like Rufus understand something that many of us miss. Culturally, we have misunderstood the concept of "balance." We aspire to balance "work" (or "things we do at an office") and "life" (or "anything we do away from the office") with the goal of making adequate time for life away from work.

Certainly, some people are overworked and need more time with family and friends. But when I see a life of fullness and significance like Rufus's, I don't think to measure it by the length of his workweek. Rather I see it as a balance of meaning and joy in *all* his activities, personal and professional.

We should all attempt to balance purpose and enjoyment in everything we do. And the goal of that balance shouldn't be a time allocation but fulfillment or flourishing—the kind of human life that comes with pleasure, happiness, achievement, and meaning seamlessly intertwined. It is not just a *happy* life (though it may be happy) but a *good* life, one lived well and for worthy

TABLE 2-1

A new framework for work-life balance

	What it means	What it looks like
Misery	The condition where one's life is dominated by activities that are both joyless and purposeless.	The person facing serious health challenges who cannot engage in meaningful or happy activities or the person who stays in a job in which they do not enjoy their day-to-day tasks and are disconnected from the purpose of their work.
Drudgery	A state in which one's actions are purposeful but joyless—life can have meaning but lacks enjoyment.	The new parent of a colicky baby who knows how important their care for the child is but struggles with exhaustion, or the emergency room doctor in a pandemic who feels the critical importance of their work but struggles with the mental and physical stress it causes.
Superficiality	The condition of engagement in enjoyable but meaningless activities—a sense that life is happy but lacks any dedication to a cause greater than oneself.	The person who enjoys life but lives only for himself or the person with shallow relationships who engages in fun activities but never serves a higher purpose or develops meaningful friendships.
Flourishing or fulfillment	The sense that most activities in life are both reasonably enjoyable and dedicated to some meaningful purpose.	The person who enjoys their relationships with their family and friends, feels connected to the meaning and purpose of their work, engages regularly in serving others, and pursues challenging but happy avocations.

purposes. You can think of it as a balance as shown in figure 2-1.

Enjoyable things are those which are fun, pleasurable, or entertaining. Purposeful things are those that offer a sense of meaning, depth, or direction—the "why" in your work. Purpose looks different for different people. Some may find it in perfecting a craft, serving others, creating something new, or contributing to a team—but whatever

FIGURE 2-1

Flourishing people balance purpose and enjoyment

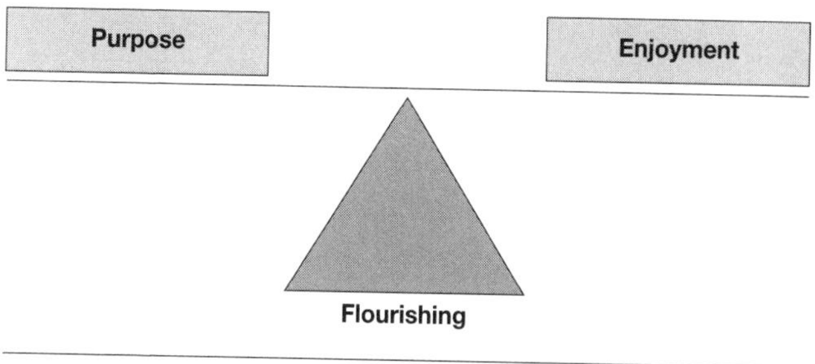

its manifestation, purpose is the thing that gives your work and life a sense of impact and importance. Some things can be enjoyable but not purposeful—a swim on a hot summer day, for example. And some things can be purposeful but not enjoyable, like childbirth or a new diet. But each is necessary to a fulfilled and flourishing life.

All of our most engaging activities, personal and professional, have elements of both purpose and enjoyment. At home, for example, I have a number of responsibilities that are meaningful but not enjoyable: changing diapers, doing loads of laundry, hanging curtains. If my personal life were made up of only these things, I'd never want to go home. They're not fun, and they're the price I pay for the privilege of being a husband and father—fulfilling because they are purposeful. But there are a lot of fun activities, too—things I *want* to do: jumping on the trampoline with my kids, going to concerts with my wife, having dinner discussions with good friends. These things are joyful as well as purposeful.

Similarly, at work, we all have responsibilities—certain committee meetings, difficult conversations with colleagues, and so on—that are essential to achieve personal growth or the mission of the organization. These are the necessary evils we take on as part of our purposeful commitment to our workplaces, our colleagues, and the objectives of our work. And then there are the fun parts—lively problem-solving sessions, innovation, synthesizing new concepts or ideas in writing. We accept the sacrifices because they must be done for our own good or the good of others. And we embrace the activities that bring us joy because they energize us.

We can conceive of the basic ways we see this balance play out in our lives in a two-by-two grid as seen in figure 2-2—with the right balance leading to flourishing and imbalances making us fall short. You can think of each quadrant in the following ways:

- **Drudgery:** Have you ever felt that your life—at work and at home—was all responsibility and no joy? At the office you may feel like you're stuck only doing things you must do, rather than anything you enjoy. At home, you're caught running errands, doing housework or dealing with problems rather than enjoying friends, family, or hobbies. These aren't meaningless activities—they have to be done and are important. But they are not joyful. This is drudgery: It may have purpose, but it's joyless and draining.

- **Superficiality:** Alternatively, imagine a life with no meaningful responsibilities. It might sound

FIGURE 2-2

2x2 for crafting a purposeful and joyful life

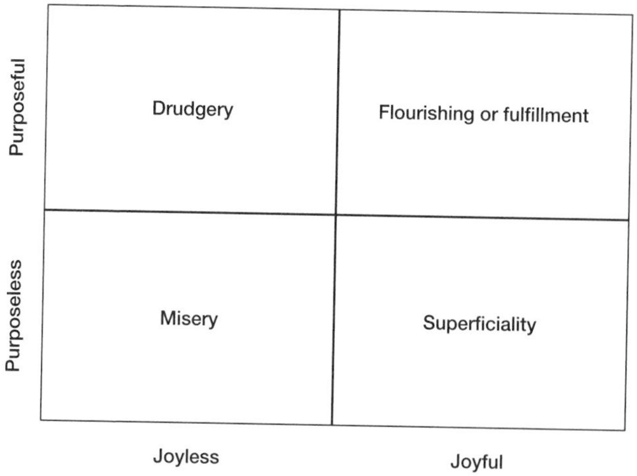

	Joyless	Joyful
Purposeful	Drudgery	Flourishing or fulfillment
Purposeless	Misery	Superficiality

wonderful. But flitting from interest to interest without really sacrificing anything or taking on the burdens of others would end up being hollow and superficial—an easy but shallow and purposeless existence. Unless we feel that we are uniquely needed, we end up empty and wanting more.

- **Misery:** Worst of all would be to live without joy or purpose—rudderless and unhappy all at once. We may engage in activity, but it doesn't seem uniquely meaningful and it's not fun. As bad as this sounds, this is the place many people feel they occupy. It's the mom or dad who doesn't feel particularly needed by their family but also doesn't feel happy or needed at work. It's the employee punching the clock without really knowing why.

It's the person who's achieved their version of success but found it emptier than they hoped it would be. Fortunately, I believe that most people who feel this way are actually in error. Their lives have the remarkable potential for purpose . . . they just haven't realized it yet and mined the meaning in their lives.

- **Flourishing or fulfillment:** Best is to live a life that combines purposeful commitment to self (through character-building and self-improvement) and to others—enriched by the joy of friends, fulfilling hobbies and professional pursuits, and meaningful time with loved ones. This kind of life is flourishing and fulfilling.

This framework is a helpful tool because it allows you to think through the things you're doing daily or weekly and where they fit on the grid. Everything can't fall in the upper-right quadrant—that's a fantasy. But if the quadrants are too out of balance, you know it's time to make changes. It also helps you to see where you need to either drop certain activities or change the way you approach them to make them more meaningful and enjoyable.

What Kind of Life Are You Leading?

Where does your life fall on the grid? Jot down the 10–20 daily or weekly activities you take on—financial reports, soccer games, committee meetings, and dinner preparation—and place them in the appropriate box. Where do the bulk of your activities lie? Are there changes you need to make? What would it look like if your life were lived in the upper-right-hand "flourishing" box? The structured thinking you're doing now will help lay the foundation for future exercises that will drive us further and further into more meaningful activities throughout our life.

Core to this framework is purpose. Without purpose and meaning woven into everything we do, even the most enjoyable of lives will fall short of flourishing. And the darker, less enjoyable moments will be nearly impossible to bear. That's where we as a society and as individuals often go wrong. We know we want to enjoy life, but we miss opportunities to make it significant. Purpose—in its infinite diversity of forms—is essential to living well.

Unfortunately, the topic of purpose is dominated by three myths that make meaning more difficult to realize. Deconstructing those myths—as we will do in the next section—is critical to crafting purpose.

SECTION TWO

Redefining How We Think About Purpose

CHAPTER 3

Dispelling Three Common Myths

"How do I find my purpose?"

That was the first question at my first book event after publishing *Passion and Purpose* in 2011. I was speaking at the COOP in Harvard Square—the university's main bookstore—to a group of perhaps 50–60 people. The crowd was incredibly diverse, and the young woman who asked the question looked to be an undergraduate student perhaps 20 years old in a grey sweatshirt. At the time, I remember stumbling through the answer. I don't remember what I said. I know she must have left as unsatisfied with my answer as I was.

But the young woman's question stuck with me—and it wasn't the last time I was asked it. Every speech after that, I got a version of the same question. And every time I responded, I was forced to consider it anew.

I've come to believe that the question is so difficult to answer because it is fundamentally flawed. It is packed with at least three beliefs that immediately lead us down an unhelpful path and away from realizing meaning in our work. That's not a criticism of my young questioner or the many who followed her—I held the same misconceptions.

After years of wrestling with the topic, I've discovered there are three myths we must confront in how we think about purpose:

1. **Purpose is something we find.** We believe it is a pot of gold at the end of the rainbow or a buried treasure. The reality is that purpose is mined and made, not found.

2. **Purpose is a single thing.** That young woman, as so many of us do, asked about her "purpose"—singular—presumably the one thing that would give her life meaning. But I've come to believe meaning is plural, not singular, and almost infinitely so.

3. **Purpose is static.** We assume we have a single PURPOSE—all caps—that is the same yesterday, today, tomorrow, and forever. The reality, more hopefully, is that our infinite opportunities for meaning shift and change dramatically over time.

Why do these myths exist? Partially, it's because we've built up romantic but misleading conceptions about purpose and meaning in popular culture. Great fiction is

TABLE 3-1

Three myths we hold about purpose

Myth	Proper conception
Purpose is a thing you find—a pot of gold at the end of a rainbow waiting for us to stumble onto it.	Purpose is a thing you mine and make—almost any activity can be meaningful if approached properly, considered thoughtfully, and crafted to enhance its purpose.
Purpose is a single thing—the one big thing that will give your life meaning.	Purpose is plural—all of us have nearly infinite opportunities for purpose in our lives, and truly flourishing people learn to find meaning in almost everything they do.
Purpose is stable over time—there's one big thing that should define your life from cradle to grave.	Purpose changes over time—while there are things in our life that are permanent or long-lasting, the multitude of ways in which we gain meaning naturally shifts as we enter new stages of life.

often predicated on a "hero's journey"—a defining quest that gives a protagonist's life meaning. And when we tell the stories of women and men who have accomplished great things—astronauts, entrepreneurs, and political leaders—we often simplify their stories to make a point. There is something romantic in that kind of unitary focus. But in buying into that falsehood we're also buying into a series of untruths that can actually make life more frustrating and unfulfilling.

Let's unpack each of these myths a little bit more, one at a time.

Myth #1: Purpose Is Something You Find

Like millions of others, I'm enjoying Disney's *Star Wars* series, *The Mandalorian*. The series centers on a mysterious figure whose life is dominated by his pursuit of fugitives. In the first episode of the series, the Mandalorian's life doesn't look very fun or purposeful.

But then he's commissioned on a particularly high bounty and discovers that his newest fugitive is an adorable, innocent baby. The Mandalorian captures this prey and hands him over to be imprisoned, abused, or slaughtered, but then has a change of heart, re-kidnaps the cute kid, and leaves town as a fugitive himself. This violent, purposeless mercenary has a purpose—saving the baby—fall in his lap.

This is not a unique literary formulation. In mythology, it's a critical part of the hero's journey—a call to adventure that sets in motion a quest by which an ordinary person becomes a hero. It's Katniss Everdeen tossed into the Hunger Games. It's Luke Skywalker pulled from his boring life on Tatooine or Rey Skywalker on Jakku. It's Frodo Baggins plucked from obscurity to confront great evil in the *Lord of the Rings*. In these constructs, the hero is leading a normal—often disappointing—life, but fate delivers to him or her one true purpose, a quest, which imbues the hero's life with meaning.

On social media, I often see an inspiring quotation attributed to Mark Twain: "The two most important days in your life are the day you are born and the day you find out why." That quote neatly articulates this Hollywood version of purpose. The problem is that for most people, that "call to adventure" never happens so clearly. And if you wait your whole life for it, or even seek out the one call to adventure that can make your life meaningful, you're almost certainly destined for disappointment not discovery.

Purpose isn't only a thing you find. More often, it's a thing you mine and make—something you weave into your existing work and life. The call to adventure is yours to craft.

Myth #2: Purpose Is a Single Thing

The second myth I often hear is that purpose can be articulated as a single thing. It's the one calling that can define a person's life—the true intersection of their talents and the world's needs. It's the "why" of their life Twain so romantically articulates. And if found, it is sufficient to fill every part of life with meaning.

On the surface some people do seem to have an overwhelming purpose in their lives. Mother Teresa lived her life to serve the poor. Samuel Johnson poured every part of himself into his writing. Marie Curie devoted her energy to science.

And yet even these luminaries had other sources of purpose in their lives. Mother Teresa served the poor as part of what she believed was a higher calling—a devotion to a faith that also called her to reflection, prayer, relationship, and study in addition to service. Curie, the Nobel laureate, was also a devoted wife and mother (she wrote a biography of her husband Pierre, and one of her daughters, Irene, was awarded her own Nobel prize). And Johnson, beyond his writing, was known to be a great humanitarian in his community, caring personally for the poor and often filling his house with the nomadic people with whom he formed close relationships. In chapter 2, we saw this in the life of Rufus Massey, who crafted multiple careers and invested in his family and barbershop quartet.

Most of us will not have one true purpose—maybe no one does. Rather, we have multiple sources of purpose in our lives. It's not *purpose* we are looking for but *purposes*—the varied sources of meaning that help us find value in our work and lives. Professional commitments are only one component of this meaning, and often our work isn't even the most meaningful thing that we do. Acknowledging these multiple sources of purpose takes the pressure off the search for a single thing to give our lives meaning.

Myth #3: Purpose Is Static

"How do I find my purpose?" When my clever respondent asked that question, she was looking for something that could guide her entire life—from that point in college through her career to the grave. But our lives aren't like that. In my own life, my purpose has shifted dramatically over time. As a young student, my world was my parents and siblings, friends, and the hobbies I enjoyed. Early in my career, it was learning the skills to thrive in business, charting a career path, traveling to new places and seeing the world, and finding a life partner. And, now, I find purpose in my job, my community activities, my wife, and my four kids—my days of high school basketball and solo travel largely in the past. In the remainder of my life, I'll likely transition careers again at some point, have grandkids, and shift more of my time to community service.

In a world in which the outside environment is so dynamic and unstable, such a shift may be more true now than ever. It's common now for people to have multiple careers in their lifetimes. I know one individual, for example, who recently left a successful private equity career to found a startup. I know two more who recently left business careers to run for elective office. And whether or not we switch careers, most of us will experience personal phases in which our sources of meaning change—childhood, young adulthood, parenthood, empty-nesting, and retirement, to name a few.

This evolution in our sources of purpose isn't flaky or demonstrative of a lack of commitment, but natural and good. Just as we all find meaning in multiple places, the sources of that meaning can and do change over time.

There's rarely one purpose that defines an entire life—or at least not only one purpose (those of religious faith, for example, may have one unifying lifelong purpose but it's not their only stable source of purpose). Rather purpose—like us—changes over time.

Moving Forward

Most of us hold onto three fundamental myths of purpose. Do they resonate with you? We'll spend the rest of this book further breaking down these myths and replacing them with more constructive concepts that will allow each of us to make meaningful changes and to craft greater purpose in each area of our life. This may not require a change in jobs, cities, or friends. But it will, at least, require a shift in mindset and a conscious effort to mine and make greater meaning in each area of our lives.

CHAPTER 4

Mining Your Life for Meaning

In his book, *House of Morgan*, legendary historian Ron Chernow tells the story of Texas Gulf Sulphur uncovering an almost unfathomably pure concentration of precious minerals. To quote Chernow:

> *In November 1963, Texas Gulf drilled a secret hole at Timmins, Ontario, that flabbergasted its chief mining engineer: it was richer than anything he had seen, richer than anything ever reported in the technical literature. This mother lode of copper, zinc, silver, and lead was later valued at up to $2 billion; it was rich enough to supply 10 percent of Canada's need for copper, 25 percent of its zinc. It was a vein so fabled that the ore sat right on the surface and could be "scooped up like gobs of caviar," as one miner said.*

Could you imagine silver or gold so pure you could literally scoop it up with your hands? It would be the proverbial "pot of gold at the end of the rainbow" made real. Miners might fantasize about such a thing—once in a while a person might actually find it; but I would never rely on the possibility.

Typical metals mining is an arduous, risky, and time-consuming affair. Copper, gold, and silver are often buried deep underground. These precious metals aren't pure and refined in their natural state but are diffuse—scattered in trace amounts through tons of waste rock and dirt. They are there, but they're hard to find. Good mining operations have to identify concentrations of the metals, they must laboriously chisel and dig for them, and then they must painstakingly refine the materials until they have a purer version of the valuable substance they seek.

That's why I prefer to think of purpose as "mined and made" not found. Sure, once in a while someone stumbles upon their "calling," just as the lucky executives of Texas Gulf stumbled upon the unfathomably rich veins of Timmins, Ontario. Tiger Woods, the greatest golfer in history, was playing nine holes at three years old and hitting balls on TV at five. Beethoven drafted his first composition at four or five years old. And some of our greatest heroes have experienced their Mark Twain moment.

But most of the rest of us are working more typical mines, where keeping our jobs meaningful day-to-day requires conscious effort. Even those of us with a "calling" fall in and out of love with it as we grow tired or disillusioned or the daily routine itself grows monotonous. If you're a pediatric oncologist, the purpose of your work may be obvious. But what if you're an accountant, cafeteria worker, or pharmaceutical sales rep? Each of those professions can have great meaning, but it takes more concentration to extract and shape it. Learning to search consciously for purpose in our work, to refresh our sources of meaning, and to witness the value of our efforts with new eyes is a constant but worthwhile struggle. And learning to employ the same techniques away from our jobs can open us to the meaning embedded in every part of our lives.

Mining Purpose—Even When It's Hard to See

In the late months of 2019 and early months of 2020, the Covid-19 pandemic erupted around the world, causing death and sickness for millions. It crippled the global economy and shut down entire countries. It would trivialize this crisis to begin broadly speaking of silver linings—we've experienced too much sickness, death, fear, and economic hardship. But as we search for rays of hope among the dark clouds, one may be the focus this crisis has thrown on the meaning and critical importance of the work so many people do.

Suddenly, with the entire world locked down and worrying about finding food to eat and receiving essential services, the jobs of delivery people, nurses, cashiers, janitors, garbagemen, and slaughterhouse workers became more obviously meaningful.

On March 19, 2020, for example, Twitter user @optundone tweeted: "Back hurts. Shoulders hurts.

TABLE 4-1

How to mine your life for meaning

	What it means	What it looks like
Conduct a survey	The process of looking through life's activities, either current or prospective, for potential sources of meaning—in the same way a surveyor looks for likely deposits of minerals.	Reflecting consciously on your life—what you are good at, what gives you flow, what moves you emotionally, where the world needs you, and those things you should avoid.
Assemble a crew	Assembling a group of peer advisors or a formal or informal board of directors who can help in the process of reflecting on, drilling for, and refining life's sources of meaning.	Pulling together four or five peers and/or mentors whom you respect, who will act in your best interest, who complement you, who will partner with you, and who can offer you wisdom you don't yet have.
Drill for meaning	The process of deep reflection on multiple areas of life to excavate all of the varied sources of meaning in those areas in preparation for crafting those activities to accentuate those sources of meaning.	Going area-by-area in your life asking yourself important questions like: Who do you serve? What do they need? How can you be a more positive influence on them, and is there more opportunity for craft in what you do?

Barely slept. Working another 12 hour day today to make sure several buildings are properly sterilized. And some ppl have no respect for us janitors." Later, in reply to another user he commented, "I hope this crisis shows us how much we need each other." During the Covid-19 crisis, janitorial work was a front-line job saving lives.

On March 14, 2020, Twitter user @justmeturtle tweeted:

> *I'm a garbageman, I can't work from home and my job is an essential city service that must get done. It's a tough job, from getting up pre-dawn to the physical*

toll it takes on my body to the monotonous nature of the job, at times it's hard to keep on going. Right now though, right now I am feeling an extra sense of pride and purpose as I do my work.

Every job in our world exists because it meets some need. But in normal times, that need can be hidden and easy to overlook. In the day-to-day grind of life, the meaningful elements don't simply rest on the surface of your jobs like the ore in Timmins. Like the more typical deposits of precious metals scattered all over the world every day, they must be mined.

So how does one mine a profession and a life for purpose? Helpfully, it is a repeatable process. To mine your own life and work for purpose, take three simple steps: conduct a survey, assemble a crew, and drill for meaning.

Conduct a survey

Any attempt to make work and life more purposeful requires looking in the right places. The idealist admonition to "do what you love" isn't really practical. Many of us aren't quite sure what we love or that we love any one thing enough to make it the center of our lives. Some of us know something we'd love to do but simply aren't good at it (hence my nonexistent musical career). And some us love to do something but can't make devoting ourselves to that thing align with our other meaningful goals. Working as a management consultant and constantly traveling, for example, may run counter to the desire to be present for children. Finally, many of us simply don't have the financial freedom or professional opportunity to do what we love and must work jobs that have dignity but aren't glamorous.

But taking a job in contradiction to one's values or where one is likely to be unsuccessful and anguished is counterproductive. As you start the process of mining for your professional purpose, ask a few questions to make sure you're looking in the right place.

What are you good at?

Writer and theologian Frederick Buechner is credited with saying, "Your vocation in life is where your greatest joy meets the world's greatest need." I might add that you have to be good at that thing. Take a moment to write down two to five unique talents that you have. Are you a great communicator or artist? Are you an athlete, or are you good at mediating conflict? Are you a beautiful singer or a strong mathematician? If you have a difficult time identifying your strengths, ask a family member, spouse, or close friend—others are often better at seeing our talents than we are. Understanding what you're good at can be a foundation as we begin to mine purpose as we find more purpose in work we do well. And some of these talents—from knitting to negotiations—can help you find purpose outside your work as well as inside it.

What gives you enjoyment or flow?

The American Psychological Association says a "flow" state (first proposed by psychologist Mihaly Csikszentmihalyi) arises, "when one's skills are fully utilized yet equal to the demands of the task, intrinsic motivation is at a peak, one loses self-consciousness and temporal awareness, and one has a sense of total control, effortlessness, and complete concentration on the immediate situation (the here and now)."

Sometimes we're good at things we don't enjoy or struggle to focus on. I'm reasonably good at math, for example, but I learned early in my career that I couldn't find "flow" in a job that required me to do nothing but math all day. Think back over the last 10 years. What were three to five times you felt completely engaged in an activity at work or away from work? What professional activities can you get lost in? What are you doing when you look up after hours and it feels like no time has passed? I've always loved public speaking, for example, and while it can't be all of my job, I always look for opportunities that allow me some opportunity to speak publicly. I similarly love writing, negotiations, coaching and mentoring, investing, and creating strategies. Is there overlap between the "what you're good at" list and the list of things that give you flow?

What moves you at an emotional level?

Purpose is often about helping others or making an impact on the world. What moves you? Do you enjoy making others happy? Do you love seeing other people smile? Would you rather help successful people shine brighter and realize their full potential, or are you more wired to spend your time working with those who are struggling and to see them improve? Do you love a good story, or do you revel in a beautiful equation? Knowing what moves you on an emotional level can help you understand not only where to look for purpose but how to enhance everything you do with more meaning. Write down 5–10 things that have moved you at an emotional level in the last two to three years—whether something in your profession, in your community, or in your own home. Is there a chance to act on them with your talents?

Where is there a need in the world or in your life?

You may love your hobbies. But are they needed in the world? Are there professional opportunities for what you want to do? Are you good enough to get them? Do they pay enough to support your other goals?

Look back over the list of things that you're good at, that give you flow, and that move you. Some of these things can be trivial or personal—things you do for fun but that don't make a big difference in the world. I, for one, love to doodle, but the world doesn't need my doodling and won't pay for it! But are there two or three things from your list that can fill an obvious need in the world? We can get purpose simply from being good at something or perfecting a craft. Circle a few items on your list from your talents and interests that are needed in the world. These offer a unique opportunity for impact.

Is there anything you have to steer clear of?

Finally, you want to apply a negative screen: Are there things you absolutely can't do and still live aligned with your values? Too often, I see people take jobs with companies or organizations they feel morally ambivalent toward because of the money or out of impatience or fear they won't find something else. If you are a vegan for moral reasons, you likely shouldn't work for a firm that does animal testing or makes animal products. We all make compromises in our career—we sacrifice a little purpose at work, for example, because more is not practical or in order to optimize purpose at home. But you should never do anything misaligned with your values. Doing so makes living authentically and purposefully in any area of life nearly impossible. What are the professional lines you will refuse to cross?

This initial survey can be a starting point in determining the most purposeful areas in which you can conduct your work. It can be done to find a new job. It can help establish more purposeful options within your existing work. It can also help you spot opportunities for purpose in your broader life. Once you've completed this survey, talk about it with someone close to you—perhaps even members of the "crew" we identify next.

Assemble a crew

While the image of a solitary prospector sifting through sediment to find gold endures, real mining is a team activity. And it's nearly impossible to effectively mine your life and work for purpose without some support.

For many of us the beginnings of this support are natural—our spouses or partners, our friends, our family, and those who care for us. Those closest to us can be the most supportive and encouraging and see things in our lives that we do not. Engaging them in a conversation about the sources of purpose in our lives can be invaluable. But it can also be limiting if your closest supporters don't offer diverse perspectives, so it's important to pick people who want you to succeed but aren't afraid to hold you accountable and think differently than you.

For these reasons, it also helps to assemble a group of advisers with more distance and more structure than a core group of family and friends. One form this more structured group can take is a personal board of directors, an idea advocated by Priscilla Claman, president of Career Strategies, among others. A personal board of directors is a group you consult for guidance and feedback in your professional efforts—and they can be just as useful in helping to articulate sources of meaning in our work and lives as in accelerating your career.

Alternatively, Bill George, the former CEO of Medtronic and a professor at Harvard Business School, has written of support networks he calls "true-north" groups. In his words, such a network should consist of, "a small, intimate group of peers who talk openly about personal and professional issues as well as their beliefs, values, and principles in a confidential setting."[1] These collectives differ from boards of directors in that they are two-way: each member helps the others. And they can manifest in different ways: religious people congregating for faithful support, or entrepreneurs meeting to share in the trials and tribulations of the startup life. But the groups share a dedication to one another, a vulnerability with one another, and a focus on helping and holding accountable to one another.

As you form your own personal board of directors or true-north group to help you identify your purpose, consider a few questions to ensure you're assembling the right minding crew. Using these questions, identify three to five people (as well as two backups) who fit your criteria and might be willing to help you think through your purpose.

Whose perspective do you respect enough to listen to?

It seems rudimentary, but if you're going to seek advice and counsel from someone you need to respect them. Whose life do you admire? Who do you look up to? Who do you see flourishing and happy in their lives, living with meaning and purpose? Think about those who seem to have crafted careers you respect, who have behaved with honesty and integrity, who have positive relationships with those closest to them, and who are happy. It's easier for a person who knows what it means to live with purpose to help you find and cultivate sources of purpose in your own life.

Who will think and act with your best interest in mind?

Not everyone is on your side. Some people are jealous or highly competitive. Some are self-involved and can only see their own interests or suffer from the zero-sum bias of viewing your gain as their loss. Some simply don't have time. For your board of directors or true-north group, think of people who are capable of empathizing with you, understanding you, and keeping your best interest in mind.

Who will complement your personality and help you see things in new and interesting ways?

We're at our best when we're listening to diverse perspectives. Who do you admire who is different than you? Can you find people who can illuminate different aspects of your work or life and provide complementary perspectives? To compel some diversity, try to find individuals from at least two or three different areas of your life—college, grad school, your current work, an old job, your social circles, or a community organization you're involved in. These people will have seen you in different contexts. Similarly, think through individuals from different backgrounds than yours, people of another gender or race, or who have contrasting personality traits that might help round your perspective. Are you risk averse? It's good to have some mentors who share that trait, but it's also wise to have at least one who's more comfortable with risk. Are you extroverted? Include at least one person in your camp who can share the introvert's perspective.

Which peers can challenge you and partner with you for life?

If you elect to select peers to either your board or true-north group, ask yourself whom among these you respect. These are not the "yes" people in your life—those who affirm you no matter what and can often lead you to poor decisions, but instead those who are willing to challenge and push you even when it's uncomfortable. Who are the peers who inspire you to improve and are constantly pushing themselves to be better? Who will hold you accountable when you're not living up to your own standards? As you select these people, it will be important for them to understand your aspirations and personal standards and for you to explicitly empower them to challenge you when you stray. For example, I have several peers who hold me accountable for how I behave as a husband and dad—people whose own behavior I respect and who feel empowered to challenge me if I fall short of my own standards.

Who might offer wisdom and experience that you have yet to acquire?

For either a board of directors or a peer group, target those with the wisdom and experience you hope to acquire. Who has it figured out? Who, despite success or age, still seeks to grow? Who despite the twists and turns of life still seems fulfilled and content? These people could be older or younger than you. All will have at least some life experiences you have yet to acquire.

Email or call these people over the next month and ask them if they might be willing to spare an hour over the phone or in person now and again to help you reflect on your work and your purpose. You can do this one-on-one or collectively (though one-on-one is right for most people).

Drill into the raw materials

So, you've found fertile ground. You've got the right crew. Knowing yourself and having a team to advise you are the key precursors to mining more purpose from your everyday experiences. Now what? The next step, naturally, is to get to the hard work of mining itself—drilling into the raw material of your life or profession in search of the bits of that life that can make it more meaningful and complete.

Much of the rest of this book will focus on the process of drilling for the raw material of meaning and converting it into something purer and more precious (see section 3). But as you embark on your journey of mining and making purpose, consider a few concluding questions that might help you zero in on the richest places to drill.

Articulate answers to each of the questions in this section, particularly related to your primary job or community activities. Make sure to have three to five answers to each question as we'll return to these topics later.

Who do you serve in your day-to-day work?

Purpose is often primarily about helping others. Who do you serve? In some fields this is easy—grocery store cashiers serve those who check out with them every day. In some fields this is harder. In asset management, for example, the end client (the beneficiary of a pension program or life insurance company, for example) is often someone no one at the firm will ever meet. But identifying that client and understanding more about them can help drive better work and connect us more deeply to a mission of working for them. Some "clients" may even be colleagues—for the technology expert, for example, who serves both the external clients of his company and the internal colleagues with whom he or she works.

What do those people need?

It's important to really sit down and ask yourself: What do the people I serve need? If you're a cashier, your clients certainly need you to ring up their items and charge them the proper amount. But dig deeper. Many who pass by a cashier need affirmation, friendliness, speed, and a thousand other things. Digging into the deeper and more existential needs of those you serve can reveal a rich vein of purpose. Who do you most serve on a day-to-day basis? With that person in mind, write a free-form list of at least three to five things you think they need from the personal (for example, affirmation and encouragement) to the professional (on-time delivery of a product). With list in hand, can you start to see the person you serve more holistically? Are there other people you serve whom you could see this way?

How can you be a positive influence on your colleagues?

In business, at least, we're often very good at serving clients—they are our lifeblood and keep any firm alive. But we are often poor at serving each other as colleagues. We can neglect our coworkers or even treat them transactionally in the mad rush to meet client needs or achieve our own goals. The people you work with, however, are still people who desperately want to be respected, treated kindly, listened to, and valued. Who are the people you work with? What are their needs? How can you serve them as well?

Where, in your work, is there the opportunity for "craft"?

Not all purpose is external—it's not all about serving others. I believe there can be great purpose in a job well done, in the fulfillment one finds in improving upon and perfecting a craft. I once worked with an analyst at McKinsey who took great pride in her PowerPoint presentations—that they were simultaneously crisp, clear, and beautiful. She would agonize over minor improvements until she felt they were perfect and felt deep satisfaction in a job well done. What are the activities you do at work that offer an opportunity for craft? They can be a unique place to mine for purpose.

Table 4-2 provides an example of this activity for Cathy, an HR benefits manager. In completing this exercise, Cathy may discover new opportunities to serve others, new needs she is meeting she'd never recognized, an opportunity for excellence in her work, and a broader sense of meaning in the things she's already doing in her life.

Your own answers to these questions will reveal veins of purpose that could be fruitful to mine. But mining alone isn't enough to imbue your life with purpose. You must also take these raw materials and craft them into something beautiful.

TABLE 4-2

Cathy's worksheet for mining the raw materials of your work for meaning

Question	Three to five initial thoughts
Who do you serve in your day-to-day work?	• My colleagues at the company who rely on me to navigate complex topics, sometimes in difficult circumstances • The families they support with our benefits • Our vendors, who often deal with upset customers and unreasonable demands
What do those people need?	• Colleagues and their families need clear guidance on complex topics and certainty that they have what they need; they may also need education on unfamiliar topics • Sometimes they also need a steady hand and a trust-worthy person while navigating a medical or financial emergency • Our vendors need a reasonable partner who works with them, not against them
How can you be a positive influence on your colleagues?	• Go the extra mile to let them know I care, spending time with them when they are confused or uncertain • Be calm and steady in emergencies, a rock for people who are suddenly relying on their benefits • Be friendly and engaged, a positive influence on the individual lives of customers and vendors alike
Where, in your work, is there the opportunity for craft?	• Get to know potential benefits plans as well as anyone in the industry—picking the right service providers for my colleagues and knowing them well enough to communicate and train • Get to know my colleagues' needs (within constraints of privacy) so that I can be an expert counselor when needed

From Mined to Made

Plenty of people work in fields with Timmins levels of raw purpose—teaching, medicine, government service—but never choose to craft the raw material of their work into something truly meaningful. Then there are people like Curtis Jenkins who take a mine almost no one would think to quarry and turn what they find there into something beautiful and unique.

THE SLUDGE OLYMPICS

On May 2, 2019, the New York City Department of Environmental Protection kicked off the 32nd annual Operations Challenge—aka the Sludge Olympics—a day-long competition among New York sewage treatment workers.

Made famous, by Ellen Barry's beautifully written 2007 *New York Times* article, the Challenge pits teams of wastewater treatment professionals from around New York in five events relevant to their profession, with the winners proceeding to a statewide event in the summer and those winners proceeding to a national event in the fall. The New York City winner has made the national competition 31 of the last 32 years.

With names like the Bowery Bay Coyotes, the Unflushables, and the Sludge Hustlers, the contestants (as seen on their entertaining Flickr page) are all smiles. They compete by simulating "collections"—responding to and repairing a leaking pipe while keeping it in service. They practice worker safety by rescuing a fellow employee while simultaneously checking air quality and changing a valve. They restore pumps in a simulated weather emergency, test water samples, and even get tested on their knowledge of the wastewater treatment process—a kind of *Jeopardy* for sanitation. The event is fun, and serves as both a reminder of the essential services these workers perform and the remarkable skills they deploy in doing so.

In her statement on the 2019 event, New York Water Environment Association Executive Director Patricia Cerro-Reehil noted the importance of the work:

> *How do we bring awareness to the important work water quality professionals perform 24 hours a day, seven days week? NYC DEP's Operations Challenge is one way these environmental professionals showcase the skills, perseverance, and drive that it takes to be a water resource recovery operator. These individuals have rewarding careers knowing they protect public health and the environment.*

Put more succinctly, George Mossos, one of the cheerful competitors Barry covered in her 2007 articles, said of his work, "It's enough to serve the public."[a]

Asked to identify a purposeful profession, most people wouldn't immediately think of sewage treatment. Yet millions of people around the world work in the field—one undeniably essential to the public good and requiring great skill and dedication. And at least some of them, like members of the Unflushables and Sludge Hustlers, have found a way to make their work both fun and incredibly meaningful.

a. Details on the 2019 event come from the May 2, 2019 New York DEP press release on the subject (https://www1.nyc.gov/html/dep/html/press_releases/19-031pr.shtml#.XiNb7C2ZNQI); details on the 2007 event are contained in Ellen Barry's May 9, 2007 *New York Times* article, "Working in the Sewers Is a Dirty Job, but Someone's Got to Win" (https://www.nytimes.com/2007/05/09/nyregion/09sewer.html).

Sometimes this is done at the organizational level, where a company structures an opportunity for meaning and purpose in your work (see the sidebar "The Sludge Olympics"). But often it's a very individual act. It could involve a professional working in purchasing at a large consumer goods company thinking about how to better serve her vendors and colleagues alike. Or it could be a consulting partner looking at all the varied people with whom his life intersects—clients, peers, junior colleagues, and others—mining those people and activities for meaning and crafting the interactions to be more purposeful. In some fields it's easier than others—but it's possible almost no matter what you do. There are examples in every profession and walk of life of people who take otherwise commonplace activities and make them meaningful.

For those who do—the Curtis Jenkinses and Rufus Masseys of the world—there are four critical ways to shape purpose as seen as figure 4-1.

1. **Craft your work:** "Craft" as a concept has a double meaning as we build more meaningful jobs. "Job crafting"—tweaking work to make it more engaging, fulfilling, or fun—is especially popular now, and for good reason. It is essential to craft your work, adapting your job in small ways to make it more intrinsically meaningful. This is taking the raw material you find in a job and adjusting your work to spend more time on and emphasize those elements while simultaneously making your whole job more impactful to others.

FIGURE 4-1

Four ways to shape purpose

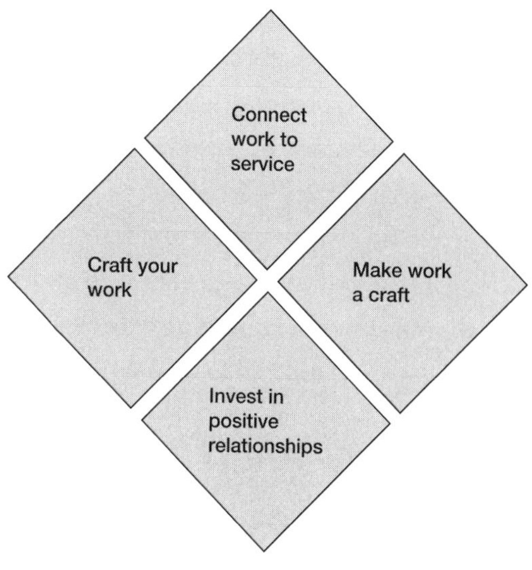

2. **Make work a craft:** Meaning also comes from treating your work as a craft—taking pride in the excellence of a job well done and becoming expert in whatever we do. One of the things most inspiring about the Operator Challenge is the pride the competitors take in their work—the expertise they deploy in repairing leaking pipes under adverse conditions. And making our work meaningful involves both job crafting and treating our work as a craft.

3. **Connect your work to service:** Research has shown definitively that we are happiest when we are serving others. And each of us, in some way, is serving someone else at work. Those in

client roles see, very clearly, that they are there to empower and serve clients. People working in technology are serving their colleagues, and those in management positions are serving those over whom they have authority. If nothing else, we're each working for some reason—to support a family, parents, friends, or causes we love, and those acts of service constitute the "why" most of us work. Finding ways to mine our daily experiences for opportunities to serve can help us generate greater meaning in everything we do.

4. **Invest in positive relationships:** Very few things matter to happiness and meaning in life as much as the relationships we have. Study upon study has shown that those who live life enmeshed in a series of positive relationships are more fulfilled and purposeful. And the need for such relationships doesn't end at the office door. The Sludge Hustlers would not be having quite so much fun without their relationships with each other, and Curtis Jenkins wouldn't be quite as fulfilled if he didn't feel a real, positive connection with his kids. While work relationships are, by necessity, of a different character than personal ones, they are essential to meaning at work. And cultivating positive relationships outside of our primary work can be the buttress that makes all our experiences more meaningful.

With these four approaches, you'll be well equipped to build a little more purpose in everything that you do—

personal and professional. And you can draw on them, too, to help you work through difficult experiences. A defense attorney may not like every client she has to defend, but she can see meaning in the system itself—offering every person accused of a crime a zealous defense. She could even see herself as a confidante to people who are suffering and encourage them to reform their lives, while choosing to reflect more consciously on the positive cases of innocent people she has freed. No job is good all the time. Some jobs are harder than others. But there is purpose in almost every job—even those with their share of negative experiences—and individuals have the opportunity to shape that purpose.

In section three, we'll explore each of these in greater detail and elaborate on how these simple habits can lead to a more purposeful life. But before moving on it's important to round out our conception of purpose realizing it's not just professional, it's personal. It's not just one thing. It's many things. And it's the type of thing that changes just as we change over time.

NOTE

1. Peter Sims, "True North Groups: A Conversation with Bill George," hbr.org, September 13, 2011, https://hbr.org/2011/09/true-north-groups.

CHAPTER 5

The Many Sources of Purpose in Your Life

Even as a child growing up in Nigeria, Ezinne Uzo-Okoro's curiosity and desire to invent was insatiable. When she found out Walt Disney slept with a pencil and paper under his pillow, she started doing the same to make sure no idea was wasted. Frustrated by the fact that she couldn't tell who was calling her house, she imagined inventing caller ID. She knew she wanted to be an inventor and a builder and, following in the footsteps of her American-educated parents, enrolled at Rensselaer Polytechnic Institute in New York. She excelled there and was headed for a PhD when she got sidetracked by an organization she'd never heard of: NASA.

At a career fair, she noticed her classmates waiting 30 minutes to speak to one particular recruiter. When she found out that recruiter wasn't even accepting résumés, she marched up and confronted him for wasting students' time. Impressed by her boldness, the recruiter took her résumé—and the rest is history. Ezinne joined the famed space organization at 20 and proceeded to chart a remarkable course. She knew that she wanted to lead teams and she wanted to try everything, so she worked hard and found ways to rotate through critical parts of the organization. By 28, she had six spacecraft launches under her belt, was lead engineer on a program with $300 million in funding, and was even selected for a special multimonth mission to the North Pole. She's grown to love space and the adventure of exploration, and she believes deeply in NASA's purpose. "It's becoming very clear to most people," she told me, "that space has been a leading frontier, not just through exploring the universe to tell us more about stars and planets, but also to protect our earth and to teach us about our planet." And she's passionate not only about pressing the frontiers of humanity in space but using space to protect people from things like hurricanes and famine here on earth.

Casual acquaintances of Ezinne might think of exploring space as her purpose, and to some extent it is. But one of the most fascinating things about Ezinne is that she's so much more than a NASA engineer. Zoom out, and she's the founder of an agriculture startup, Terraformers, based on the interest she developed in growing food in space. She recently took a partial leave from NASA to go to MIT's prestigious Media Lab, where she's focused on robotics. And she's tacking on a degree at Harvard's Kennedy School while in Boston due to her interest in public policy and the ways in which that policy can influence the scientific causes she cares about. As a young engineer she ran marathons and became proficient at Middle Eastern dance. And at home she's happily married to a dedicated partner with whom she welcomed a son in 2019. Each of these things has purpose for her. But it's the constellation of all these things that creates a web of purpose around her whole life.

As we've noted before, there's a strain of thinking that purpose is a single thing, the "why" of your life. But while superficially inspiring, that search for a singular purpose can actually induce anxiety and disillusionment. What happens when you can't seem to find that one calling? What happens when you fail at it? And what are you missing all around you while you're obsessively looking for a single professional calling to give your whole life meaning?

Purpose isn't one big thing that gives your life meaning. It's the incredible, diverse menagerie of things that gives every life meaning every single day. Opening yourself to the multiplicity of purposes already present in your life is the surest way to shake the malaise of our current crisis of meaning. Even those who achieve great things and have a special calling often find meaning in other areas of life.

As we mentioned in the last chapter, the first step in mining your life for purpose is conducting a survey. There are a nearly infinite number of places in which purpose and meaning can live, but you can remember six particularly rich sources with the acronym LABORS.

Often when we think about purpose, we only consider our work. This framework may help you to remember that there are many sources of purpose in your life, and to look to each one individually for the opportunities to identify and craft meaning.

Love

Avocations and self-improvement

Beauty

Occupation

Religion or philosophy

Service

Each of these areas can be critical to a fulfilling and meaningful life. Let's explore each of them more fully.

Love

Perhaps the longest-running longitudinal study in the world is known as the Harvard Grant Study, one of two parallel projects of the Harvard Study of Adult Development (along with the Glueck Study). The Grant Study followed 268 Harvard undergraduates from the classes of 1939 to 1944, including John F. Kennedy Jr. and a number of other prominent American men.

George Vaillant was a principal investigator on the Grant Study and spent 30 years as the director of the Study for Adult Development. He's written three books on the Grant Study, most recently *Triumphs of Experience*, checking in on the men when they were in their

TABLE 5-1

The LABORS framework for multiple sources of purpose

	What it means
Love	"Happiness is love. Full stop." The process of finding and engaging in deep, meaningful relationships.
Avocations and self-improvement	Those things we do outside our primary occupation or profession that provide diversion, offer smaller opportunities for craft, or in other ways enrich our lives or lead to self-improvement.
Beauty	Seeking out and creating things or experiences that are beautiful—from reading or writing an elegant book to watching a sunset or painting a portrait.
Occupation	A person's primary professional pursuit at any given time—the way in which we earn a living and develop a sense of accomplishment through work.
Religion or philosophy	A religious faith or philosophic tradition that helps to interpret the world, provides a guide to the "good life," and offers the opportunity to serve a "higher calling."
Service	Selflessly using one's time, talents, and resources to help others—whether colleagues, friends, family, or the less fortunate.

eighties or nineties. His big takeaway? "The 75 years and 20 million dollars expended on the Grant Study points . . . to a straightforward five-word conclusion: 'Happiness is love. Full stop.'"[1]

Poet John Donne famously wrote that "No man is an island." And there are few things as central to human flourishing as positive relationships. One study noted that a lack of supportive relationships increased the risk of premature death from all causes by 50%—the equivalent impact of smoking 15 cigarettes per day.[2] There are different types of "love" for different types of relationships. The ancient Greeks had as many as eight types of love applying to relationships including friends, romantic partners, parents, siblings, children, casual acquaintances, and all humankind. And the potential for these relationships is all around us.

Yet we often neglect them and take them for granted. We're surrounded by people who matter to us and to the world but overlook investing in them in order to pursue a more antiseptic "calling" or a professional purpose that may or may not ever have the meaning of a good relationship.

Maybe the Beatles were right: All we need is love. Finding positive relationships and prioritizing them can be life's greatest source of meaning.

Write down the five most important relationships in your life, listing each person by name. These relationships might be positive or might need improvement, but all should be important to you and your well-being. For each person, write down your thoughts on how you can deepen and improve the relationship—actions that you can take rather than actions the other person needs to take. For each person, condense your thoughts into one or two things you can do this week to invest in the relationship. Table 5-2 shows what this exercise looks like for Dan, a mid-level manager at a CPA firm.

Look at your own exercise and see what you can draw from it. How can you invest more in your relationships? Are there any relationships not in your top five that should be?

Avocations and Self-Improvement

Why do so many inspiring people have seemingly meaningless hobbies? Why are so many accomplished people always finding new ways to improve? Why does Rufus

TABLE 5-2

Dan's relationship matrix

Five most important relationships	Ways to deepen them	Actions to take this week
Wife	• Spend more time together without the kids to reconnect • Give her more affirmation about the great job she's doing • Listen more	• Institute weekly date night • Send her an email a day with a reason I'm grateful for her
Son	• Invest more in his interests (basketball, Pokemon, Harry Potter) • Spend more quality time	• Sign up to coach his basketball team • Read Harry Potter series out loud together
Boss	• Build trust with her about my commitment • Get to know her more as a person	• Schedule dinner with spouses • Ask to take on a new task autonomously to demonstrate skill
Jim (one of my direct reports . . . struggling right now)	• Understand his current struggles • Invest in coaching and training to help him recover • Broaden his perspective about the company	• Set weekly meeting to discuss, listen, and coach • Connect him with manager in another area for mentorship
Sam (friend, going through hard time in marriage)	• Give him a chance to let off steam and get perspective • Deliver hard truth about some of the problems	• Schedule camping trip for weekend to let him relax and talk through problems

Massey like to sing competitively and play tennis even though he'll never be a professional at either? Why did Ezinne Uzo-Okoro run marathons and take dance lessons when those hours might have been more "productively" spent advancing her career as an engineer?

The truth is, most of us have avocations—hobbies and minor occupations—outside our primary occupation or profession that provide diversion, offer smaller opportunities for craft, or in other ways enrich our lives or lead to self-improvement.

There's purpose to be had in avocations and in programs of self-improvement—from bowling and sudoku to cycling and piano. While avocations don't instill the deep sense of purpose associated with meaningful professions or positive relationships, they do offer daily, easily accessible doses of purpose that can keep the mind and spirit active. One study in Japan, for example, found a decrease in mortality associated with "hobbies and purpose in life," and professor of psychology Jaime Kurtz has written about how hobbies can offer what I'd call gateways to feelings of purpose—like structure, flow, and social connection.[3] As an added benefit, if you join a knitting group or a running club you're meeting friends and finding ways to practice craft—connecting the practice of avocations to craft and meaningful relationships.

All the better when these avocations offer meaningful self-improvement. Numerous studies have shown the benefits of reading in decreasing stress and improving empathy, for example. And reading with a book club can enhance those with further mental and social development. Self-improvement through exercise or diet can have all the meaningful benefits of a hobby along with deep physiological payoff. And activities as simple as crossword puzzles may have benefits for countering certain types of dementia.

While things like woodworking or writing poetry may not save the world, they can offer the kind of steady, consistent meaning (along with connection to broader sources of meaning) that enhance an already purposeful life. They can also expand your community of love and support.

Oftentimes, though, our busy lives mean that we forget about our hobbies and side projects. Proactively make time for them. Here are a few ways I've found helpful:

- **Do what you enjoy.** Life is busy. Focus on avocations that you enjoy. If you have to grit your teeth and force something every day you will eventually lose interest. Find activities that can eventually offer you flow.

- **Set reasonable expectations.** I recently heard of a CEO who placed top five in his age bracket for an ironman competition. He did so by training 1.5 hours each day over lunch, knowing he couldn't spare more given his role as a leader and father. If you start running, two miles a day may be plenty. If you start knitting, 30 minutes in the evening may be all you can afford. Be reasonable with yourself.

- **Schedule the time.** Avocations and self-improvement initiatives are the easiest things to de-prioritize when life gets busy. Put them on your calendar—for example, blocking the time to write at 6 a.m. or exercise at 8 p.m. each day.

- **Use a tracker.** There are tons of daily-use apps like Strides available on your mobile phone. Use them to hold yourself accountable to building your hobbies into habits.

- **Create a community.** My friend Stan runs a book group of 10–15 people called Six Pillars that keeps us reading diverse books each year. The community ensures we keep going. My friends connected to me on Peloton similarly encourage me to stay with it when it gets hard.

What avocations, hobbies, or activities of self-improvement do you have in your life? Make a list. How can you incorporate these activities more thoughtfully into your life and make them more purposeful (through group activities, connection to deeper principles, connection to craft) along the way? For example, if you've started running, could you join a group that lets you run while fostering relationship or enter a competition that allows you to focus on improving? If you love to garden, is there someone in your life (a spouse, grandchild, or friend) who could sometimes join you?

Beauty

In some ways we're a society that has forgotten the importance of beauty to life's meaning even as individuals can never escape its importance.

One of my favorite books is a novella by Norman Maclean called *A River Runs Through It.* I love it for many reasons—its exploration of the relationship between fathers and sons and between faith and the outdoors, the life story of its remarkable author. But what keeps me returning again and again is the beauty of the writing and of the nature it evokes. Maclean crafts passages so stunning in language and imagery that I find myself reading them over and over, savoring them. And their beauty offers me a sense of meaning.

It is hard to quantify how beauty connects to meaning. There are studies linking beauty and happiness, certainly. But intuitively we also grasp that beautiful things bring us more than happiness—they imbue in us the sense of the transcendence and deeper purpose embedded in life. Does life feel more meaningful when you're watching a sunset? Does it feel more alive and purposeful in an art museum or while walking the cobblestone streets of a beautiful city? For me it does. These beautiful things inspire and encourage reflection.

Moreover, have you ever noticed that there's even greater purpose when you can create a thing of beauty, not simply witness it. My wife, for example, has been taking singing and guitar lessons and gets remarkable fulfillment from the beauty of the music she's now able to produce (only enhanced by the fact that she's sharing the guitar lessons with our son). Combining the need to create beauty with the meaningful nature of hobbies could lead one to a watercolor or gardening or poetry class. Combining it with service could lead one to help clean up trash in a neighborhood or river or to invest in an arts nonprofit.

Many people in demanding professions or with busy home lives seemingly lose a sense of beauty in their lives. A high-powered corporate attorney, for example, may feel so underwater responding to client needs she forgets to pause and reflect on the paintings in the halls of her office or on the skyline outside. And an overworked parent may be so busy feeding and transporting kids they forget to make time to simply sit and laugh with them—to appreciate the unique beauty of who they are. There is beauty in almost everything if we choose to see it. That beauty is different for all of us—some may see it in soaring mountain views while others in photographs of rusty tractors or books of poetry. And all of us have the opportunity to introduce more into our lives—through museum visits or nature walks, for example—if we try.

Write down the three to five greatest sources of beauty in your life—your kids, your partner, art, the outdoors—and what makes them so beautiful. If you feel that there's not enough beauty in your life, what can you do to make the time to seek new sources of it? Identify two or three things you can do this month to seek more beauty in your life. This might be clearing some of your children's after-school activities to make more time with them or committing to attending a concert once per month. Or look for smaller ways to add these activities more regularly to your calendar without the larger time commitment, like listening to music with headphones on 20 minutes per day, lighting a candle while working, or reading a novel for half an hour before bed each night.

Occupation

Work isn't simply one place in which we can find purpose. It's central. For many of us, work is where we spend most of our time, more time than anywhere else in our lives, so making it meaningful is essential to balancing purpose and joy for a flourishing life.

More deeply, however, the act of work itself should be a source of meaning and self-respect for everyone who does it. If you are working and being paid for your work, it's because you are meeting a need. What you do is valuable to someone. That someone may be hard to see, and the work may be difficult, draining, or physically taxing. But it has dignity. It has purpose. And in doing it, you're bringing something valuable into the world. That may seem small or trite. Many people desire not the simple daily purpose of work itself but the grand meaning of a calling. But when push comes to shove, there's great value in doing something good—even something small—for the world.

Take this opportunity to simply pause for a minute or two and reflect on what you're learning so far about what makes your work meaningful. We'll explore this in much greater depth in section 4, but are there three to five elements of your work that you are most proud of, things that you see as making a difference to someone in the world? Is there anything at work that you feel you do particularly well and with craft?

Religion or Philosophy

Around 84% of the world affiliate with some religion. The four largest religions—Christianity (31.2%), Islam, (24.1%), Hinduism (15.1%), and Buddhism (6.9%)—are followed by roughly 77% of the world, or 5.7 billion people.[4] Not all those who affiliate with a religion have the same levels of faith, but the majority of people in the world to varying extent derive their values, morals, and principles—so central to purpose—from their religious traditions. Beyond the values by which people seek meaning, religion can be a source of relationship for believers—whether through a "personal relationship with God," as some Evangelical Christians believe, or through the complex relationship between the believer and the universe, as described in Buddhism. Purdue graduate researcher Jong Hyun Jung, for example, found that a sense of divine involvement increases meaning in life among Christians, and while his research didn't extend to other faith traditions one could extrapolate that they would.[5] Indeed, the majority of people I interviewed for this book expressed some connection between their own purpose-making and their religious traditions.

Further, many nonreligious people—the 16% in the Pew research above who claim no affiliation (or indeed, the high number of those who claim religious affiliation but practice no faith)—have an intense dedication to a life philosophy or a way of making meaning that provides similar orientation and connection to others. The topic has been explored extensively by many of history's greatest philosophers from Immanuel Kant to John Stuart Mill. Research indicates that the vast majority of atheists see some purpose in life, and one study even indicated belief in meaning in life is roughly equal between those with religious faith and those without it.[6]

What does this mean? Simply that it's common and constructive to mine one's religious or philosophic tradition for meaning—whether using the values inherent in those traditions (for example, service to others, connection to nature, etc.) to mine our lives for meaning or finding meaning in the relationship between ourselves and a higher power. Explicitly reflecting on the meaning and purpose you derive from your religious or philosophic practice and similarly reflecting on how it manifests in your other activities and relationships can be a powerful tool for creating coherence and purpose in your life broadly.

What system of philosophy, belief, or religious tradition helps you interpret the world? For some people, this will be easy to identify. For others, it may require more thought. After you've identified your religious or philosophic tradition, write down what it says about living a good and meaningful life. If you don't know, research it until you feel confident in articulating a paragraph or two about how your tradition connects to purpose. Similarly, jot down three to five ways in which you can apply that framework more explicitly to key activities or relationships in your life.

Service

Julissa Carielo loves construction. Julissa's parents emigrated from Mexico to Texas before she was born, and she is one of nine siblings. She'd never really considered college until, as a 16-year-old, she ended up on a community soccer team with a number of older professional women—lawyers, teachers, accountants, and advertising executives—who inspired her.

Julissa got her accounting degree from St. Mary's University and joined the finance organization at a construction firm. She rose to controller, CFO, and VP of finance and administration. But in 2006, at 35, she realized she needed a change. With no fallback options, Julissa pulled $75,000 out of her 401(k) started her own construction firm.

She lights up when she talks about her work, which is about more than buildings—it's about community service.

> *I like doing projects that are community-driven. If they're going to provide a better space for the community, I love those kind of projects. . . . I'm always pushing for the utilization of our local businesses because we need to continue to grow our own here. . . . They're our neighbors. Why wouldn't we help them first?*

While Julissa loves her work and finds it meaningful, she always felt something was missing. Just as those women from her soccer team had helped inspire her to her dreams, she wanted to help, inspire, and serve other underserved entrepreneurs. In 2016, Julissa used earnings from her successful business to start the Maestro Entrepreneur Center in San Antonio.

> *[W]hen the company turned 10 years old, I decided to purchase an [unused] elementary school to start a nonprofit—the Maestro Entrepreneurship Center to start incubating and accelerating companies. I started bringing in maestros—who are successful business owners here in San Antonio—to give back and teach. . . . We do a lot of training in that way, and we do it in all industries. The center has a building designated to each type of industry. We have a building*

> *for construction. We have one for the culinary. We have one for professional services. . . . We just have all kinds of events that helps our businesses connect to the community and for the community to get to know them. And then we offer small group training sessions and one-on-one mentorship.*

The center is dedicated specifically to helping veterans, women, and minorities who are small business owners grow and expand their businesses. Julissa thinks of her construction work as a service to her employees and her community and the Maestro Entrepreneur Center as a way to deepen that service.

Volunteering and community service are part of almost any purposeful person's life. If you make a list of the most purposeful, flourishing people you know, I'm almost certain that somewhere central to their lives is volunteer work. It may manifest in different ways; hands-on service in places like soup kitchens or nursing homes, board memberships at nonprofits, philanthropy, or simply person-to-person service offering meals to neighbors and a helping hand to those in need. But, in some way, almost every meaningful life contains service.

Active volunteering is associated with decreased mortality and higher self-esteem and happiness.[7] In a survey, 96% of respondents reported volunteer work enhanced their sense of purpose and 94% noted it raised their self-esteem, and the same survey reported a connection between volunteering and better health, low stress, and better mood.[8] Service isn't just "volunteering"—as we've explored you can serve colleagues, family members, your church, or a host of others. But I'd presume those acts of service would yield the same positive outcomes as the types of volunteering these researchers studied.

Shockingly, however, many people silo their lives—seeking their one true purpose in a professional calling while never reflecting on the intense meaning their work in the community can bring. Most people are active in their communities and helpful to friends yet fail to reflect on the importance of that service or relegate it to second class, behind finding meaning in work. For many people, volunteer work, helping others, and investing in friends and family are the primary ways in which they give and receive meaning in their lives. If you're the type of person who is active in this way, take the time to reflect on the positive impact you are having in the lives of others. If on reflection, you realize you're not investing much in others, perhaps it's time to consider how you can consciously carve out more time and energy for service.

Write down all your meaningful volunteer activities and all the ways you serve others away from work (we'll explore service at work more later in the book). Let this list be as long as needed, whether you can think of three acts of service or a hundred. Include not just formal volunteer activities but the little things you do for others—calling a relative to check in, helping a friend move, or even babysitting a niece or nephew. If your list is long, how can you better make time to reflect on and appreciate the positive impact you are having? If your list is short, write down two or three opportunities you might have to serve others this month and how you can more consistently prioritize service to others in your life.

Meaning in Every Area of Life

We all need multiple sources of purpose in our lives to truly flourish. Learning to see those sources and to invest in each can lead to more vibrant, fulfilling lives. The "LABORS"—love, avocations, beauty, occupation, religion or philosophy, and service—are central sources of meaning that almost any person can access and cultivate. These few examples also help to remind us that even when we feel most hopeless or meaningless, there's generally purpose—real purpose—in our lives.

If you're feeling particularly challenged by the lack of calling in your life, review the above. When you're mining for meaning, take an expansive view. Most of us think of purpose too narrowly as a professional pursuit when the reality is that opportunities for purpose exist in every area of your life. Are there ways in which you're shortchanging the variety of experiences that give your life meaning and by which you are creating meaning for others? I suspect there are. Don't lose sight of the sources of purpose all around you every day.

As a final exercise, review your responses from this chapter with members of your crew or with someone close to you. Have an honest conversation about the plural sources of purpose in your life—and where you could invest more.

NOTES

1. Scott Stossel, "What Makes Us Happy, Revisited," *The Atlantic*, May 2013, https://www.theatlantic.com/magazine/archive/2013/05/thanks-mom/309287/.

2. Harvard Health Publishing, "The Health Benefits of Strong Relationships," August 6, 2019, https://www.health.harvard.edu/newsletter_article/the-health-benefits-of-strong-relationships.

3. Kimiko Tomioka, Norio Kurumatani, and Hiroshi Hosoi, "Relationship of Having Hobbies and a Purpose in Life with Mortality, Activities of Daily Living, and Instrumental Activities of Daily Living Among Community-Dwelling Elderly Adults," *Journal of Epidemiology* 27, no. 7 (2016): 361–370; Jaime L. Kurtz, "Six Reasons to Get a Hobby," *Psychology Today*, September 15, 2015, https://www.psychologytoday.com/us/blog/happy-trails/201509/six-reasons-get-hobby.

4. Conrad Hackett and David McClendon, "Christians Remain World's Largest Religious Group, But They Are Declining in Europe," Pew Research Center, April 5, 2017, https://www.pewresearch.org/fact-tank/2017/04/05/christians-remain-worlds-largest-religious-group-but-they-are-declining-in-europe/.

5. Massarah Mikati, "How a Relationship with God Gives Life Meaning," *Deseret News*, June 22, 2015, https://www.deseret.com/2015/6/22/20566979/how-a-relationship-with-god-gives-life-meaning#looking-to-become-happier-many-studies-show-this-can-be-achieved-by-becoming-religious.

6. Ross Pomeroy, "Where Do Atheists Get Meaning in Life?," RealClearScience, February 1, 2018, https://www.realclearscience.com/quick_and_clear_science/2018/02/01/where_do_atheists_get_meaning_in_life.html.

7. Ben Schiller, "Volunteering Makes You Happier," Fast Company, September 3, 2013, https://www.fastcompany.com/3016549/volunteering-makes-you-happier.

8. Hillary Young, "Why Volunteering Is So Good for Your Health," HuffPost, November 1, 2013, https://www.huffpost.com/entry/benefits-of-volunteering_b_4151540.

CHAPTER 6

Embracing Shifts in Purpose

Jeff Heck is the cool guy many of us want to be. Jeff is a former rock musician who often wears his wispy blond hair pulled back in a bun and runs one of the trendiest craft breweries in Atlanta. I'd guess Jeff has always been cool, but his life and purpose have emerged in stages.

As a kid he was a sponge, and his purposes were learning, exploration, fun, and adventure. His dad was a doctor in Hicksville, Ohio, who took the family on a one-year medical mission to Kenya before returning to another small town in the Cincinnati suburbs. In his childhood Jeff learned the lessons that would become the scaffolding of his own unfolding life: family, faith, hospitality, curiosity, and commitment.

In college, things shifted. In Jeff's words:

At Harvard, it was an interesting transition because of all these things I had been involved in, and I'd been in the same smallish suburbs for 12 years. When I went there, no one knew who I was. No one knew anything about me. It was, in some ways, a little bit of a scary time as I sort of looked inward and had to ask the question, "What am I really all about?"

His purpose became exploration, of himself and the world around him. He sampled social and academic circles broadly, discovered a love of psychology, met his future wife Hannah, and began playing music more seriously. All that exploration naturally created some confusion about his future course. In his words, he could, "One, go to medical school. Two, go to seminary. Three, take my rock band on the road. Four, do something in business, which was sort of a vague black box." Yet somehow this psychologist, rock musician, and would-be seminarian ended up at Home Depot with a job in finance after school.

The next decade became about commitment and community. He worked hard at Home Depot, learning a craft in finance, before transitioning to a private equity firm called Roark Capital. Hannah and Jeff had kids—four in all—including a beautiful boy named Teddy who has Down syndrome. Jeff became not just a dad, but a great dad.

Simultaneously, the seeds of another major change were planted. During this period, Jeff was in a small Bible study group that met on Monday nights, and on a whim he and the other group members decided to start brewing beer while they met. "Before too long," Jeff says, "we were brewing more beer than a Bible study, in good conscience, could consume by itself. So, neighbors and coworkers started coming over." For four years, that brewing became a way for Jeff to meet friends and neighbors and build community. Then, in 2011, he and his friends decided to build it into a business—Monday Night Brewing, with Jeff as CEO.

What started as a hobby now occupies two large breweries in Atlanta. Monday Night's beer is in Target and in bars and restaurants all over the Southeast. Its physical spaces are hip and permanently crowded. If you visit, however, what you immediately notice is that the business is about much more than brewing. Its purpose statement, which the founders articulate as "the fundamental reason why we exist" is "[T]o deepen human relationships over some of the best beer in the country." And almost everything about the physical plants reinforce that point. There are large communal spaces in the breweries that individuals and organizations can rent and that are often donated to charities to host events. In the original facility, The Garage, mangled neckties hang from the wall, left by patrons who have cut them off—a tradition. In the newest facility, there's a wall on which patrons write messages.

What is Jeff's purpose? His family? His community? Monday Night Brewing? Jeff's story is ours. It demonstrates a fundamental truth—many of the most purpose-driven people alive not only don't have a single purpose, but they don't have a stable purpose. As they mature, so do their sources of meaning. Some are indelible. Some are relevant for a while and then fade. And some manifest differently as we grow.

How to Navigate Changing Purpose

"How do I find my purpose?"

I'd wager you already have—that you have identified, shaped, and abandoned many purposes over your life. And that natural process of growth and evolution can be rejuvenating. Just as in the last chapter we learned that we all have many sources of purpose large and small, here, we begin to understand, accept, and welcome the way our various purposes are birthed, live, evolve, and (sometimes) fade away.

Purpose changes over time. This happens in small ways, when we shift our hobbies or our interests. It happens in our relationships, in the arc from daughter to independent woman to mother, or in the evolution of a friendship. It happens as people progress along their career path or as they transition between multiple different careers entirely. And external circumstances or life events can make us rethink what purpose and meaning really is.

Dealing with these shifts can be challenging. Feeling the meaning slip from an activity or a person can cause anxiety. Knowing when to double down on something and when to leave it behind can be a delicate balance. And knowing how to identify the next source of meaning can be hard.

In the remainder of this chapter, I offer a simple four-part framework for navigating changing purpose. The "Embracing change worksheet" at the end of this chapter offers a template for you to use, so you can see answers all in one place.

TABLE 6-1

Navigating changing purpose

	What it means	What it looks like
Identify what's permanent	Commitments in life that are nonnegotiable, permanent sources of meaning. They are life's anchors.	These typically include one's faith or philosophic tradition, spouse, children, and mental or physical health. For some this may include a vocation or calling, but for many it will not.
Pay attention to transitions	Natural periods of transition in life during which one's sources of purpose and meaning are likely to shift.	This can include the big shifts in life—expected and unexpected—like high school graduation, college graduation, marriage, childbirth, starting a new job, getting laid off, retiring, having grandkids, or embarking on a new career.
Reject stagnation	Refusing to accept extended periods of boredom, monotony, and drudgery.	Seeking to reinvent a job that has become monotonous through job crafting and making work a craft, engaging a new avocation or hobby, making new friends or developing new professional relationships, and seeking new challenges.
Learn to let go	Recognizing when an activity is no longer purposeful or joyful or when it is simply time to move past it to a new stage of life.	Quitting a sport that is now physically impossible, quitting a job or switching careers, leaving behind a relationship that is no longer constructive, switching hobbies once one has been mastered.

Identify what's permanent

I once had a mentor ask me, "What's the only job only you can ever do?" His answer: being the biological parent to my children. And it's true. My wife could find a new husband. My employer could find someone better than me at my job. But my kids will only ever have me as their biological dad. And for me, my commitment to them is permanent. It's a source of meaning that I've decided in advance is important to me and that I can never abandon. The same for my religious beliefs, marriage, mental and physical health, and a handful of other commitments in my life that are nonnegotiable, permanent sources of meaning. We each have these, but it is important to identify these consciously and to regularly invest in them. The way I mine these experiences for meaning may change. My marriage looks different now than 10 years ago. And my role as dad will change meaningfully as my children age. But my challenge in each of these spheres is adapting and evolving the nature and purpose of the role, not the role itself.

What are your nonnegotiables? My wife, a psychologist, calls our commitment to the things "decision love" because that commitment isn't based on how we feel or what's going on at the time. It's based on a decision made in advance. These permanent commitments should be sparse. But they are important.

Think about what anchors you in life. (There are no points for originality.) For many people this will include being a devoted spouse or partner, loving parent, engaged friend, or faithful religious follower. For some, the list might also include a profession or avocation. I, for example, know that I want to grow as a writer throughout my life—and that commitment helps to refocus me when I'm off track. Note the permanent commitments you have that offer you meaning and purpose. These are the foundation for your meaningful life, the things that you have to keep on track no matter what. In a few minutes, beside each, jot down a few details about how on track you feel.

Pay attention to the transitions

Life is marked by big, obvious transitions. These may include graduation, a first job, new friendships, marriage and kids, selecting a career, a career transition, retirement, and many more. There may be others very specific to you—an epiphany or a health challenge that causes you to change course or an unexpected event that resets your trajectory. They are rarely subtle.

When you are transitioning, carve out some time to reconsider purpose. Almost any transition brings new sources of meaning that we should identify and learn to mine and craft. Becoming a parent or grandparent, for example, offers a life-changing source of meaning. So does losing a loved one. Graduating from college and entering the workforce—where you will be forced to think for and discover yourself independently—is a huge life transition for many that warrants regular reflection as that self-discovery occurs. Leaving a job to return to school can offer the same self-discovery. Switching a job, location, or a career warrants real thought about how to make the new role as meaningful as possible, a topic we're exploring extensively in this book.

Simultaneously, embracing this new phase and these new sources of meaning may mean letting go of something else. Any job transition, naturally, involves saying goodbye to an organization and people you invested in. Graduating means leaving friends and at least some of the reflection and exploration of education behind. Retiring from your career can feel like a loss if you're not mentally prepared to reset the way in which you craft meaning in your life. We'll explore this a bit more later in this chapter, but any change involves some embrace of the new and abandonment of the old.

Are you in a transition now? Spend some time considering the ways you mined and made meaning in the last phase of your life and how those may now change.

Reject stagnation

All of us have periods of stagnation. Sometimes these are small—we get bored with a role we are in or a project we've been assigned and find it hard to continue to invest our time and energy into it. Sometimes, these moments of stagnation are much more daunting—the infamous midlife crisis for example. Many of our most important transitions come in the first 30–40 years of life—education, dating, marriage, children, first job, defining a career. But then, for many people, there's this 20-year stretch where there aren't as many transitions taking place—where you're just investing in the career, family, and friends you've chosen. And that period can sometimes feel monotonous and stagnant.

The feeling is natural. But I don't think we ever have to accept it. The core premise of this book is that purpose is something you build, something that is multifaceted and changes over time. And that feeling of stagnation can be a gift—a signal that some "purpose crafting" is needed.

When you feel stagnant, take a moment to reflect on why. It might be that you're not feeling challenged by a job or are bored with your hobbies, or maybe you are caught up in the drudgery of your responsibilities and not making time for the enjoyment that can keep you engaged. Perhaps you're coasting and not investing in anything meaningful. That feeling of stagnation is the signal that you need to take stock of where you are and explore new opportunities for mining and making meaning in your life. (For more on how to recognize when it's time for a change, see the sidebar "Signals It's Time to Let Go.") This may be as simple as a change in the way you think about what you do or as complex as a career shift, but whatever it is it is worth pursuing if you're feeling stuck.

Stagnation is natural, but never something to accept. Make a change. If you're feeling stagnant, reflect on the following questions:

1. What am I most bored with right now? Why?
2. What am I most excited about and challenged by right now? Why?
3. Is there an area in my life where I need to take a risk? What fear is preventing me from doing so, and how might I counter that?
4. Is there an area in my life where I need to make a change?

Approaching these kinds of changes consciously and with a sense of enthusiasm can make them exciting rather than intimidating.

SIGNALS IT'S TIME TO LET GO

All of us experience moments when we must face the difficult decision to let go of doing something that formerly offered us purpose. Each person is different, and there are no hard and fast rules about evaluating when it's time to move on. Here are a few signs it might be time to let go:

- ***You regularly approach the activity with dread.*** I previously had a job that I had once enjoyed but had truly begun to wear on me, so much so that it was hard for me to leave the house to go to work in the morning. If you regularly feel dread at approaching something, it's time to seriously consider changing it or leaving it behind.
- ***You actively look for ways to avoid it.*** I had a friend who loved writing. But at some point, she had grown tired of it and began seeking ways to avoid it. She realized, ultimately, that she needed a long break from writing if she was ever going to fall in love with it again. Sometimes, you need to power through something to develop a positive habit (all of us should exercise, for example, but it can be hard to get started), but sometimes it's necessary to recognize that something has outlived its meaningfulness and take a temporary or permanent break to pick up something new.
- ***It regularly causes you physical or emotional pain.*** I stopped playing basketball because it was physically time for me to stop. Emotional or physical damage are very clear signs that something needs to change.

- ***It's no longer encouraging you to grow personally.*** The best athletes will often diversify their physical training or dramatically change their routines. This is because, at some point, everything we do too consistently ceases to be a source of growth. When you notice a source of purpose is no longer helping you grow, look to reinvention or some other change.
- ***It's causing you to develop bad habits.*** A friend of mine worked at a company whose culture was toxic, and he found himself—even away from work—behaving in ways he would have previously found unethical or inappropriate. When he recognized this, he immediately left the firm. When something you look to for purpose begins pulling you further from it, you need to let it go.
- ***You've achieved what you set out to achieve.*** A business contact of mine played in the NFL. The first phase of his life was all about football. But after he retired, he found he was satisfied with that period of his life, which had been an incredible source of meaning, and was ready to leave it behind. Sometimes we simply accomplish what we set out to achieve and are ready to move on to something new.

There are, of course, other signs. And some decisions should be approached more cautiously than others—leaving a job, for example, versus a hobby. But letting go of the old is an ever-present part of keeping life fresh and allowing purpose to change over time.

Learn to let go

During my second year of graduate school, my wife sat me down for a tough conversation. I'd just ended up on crutches—again—playing a game of pick-up basketball. Basketball had been a huge part of my life for a long time. It was the only sport I played in high school, and it had been a way I'd built community and made friends. It was my primary fitness activity, and I had practiced it for countless hours. But in the course of playing it, I had permanently damaged my ankles such that almost every time I played, I'd suffer a sprain and end up hobbled for a week or more.

In her wisdom, my wife could see what I couldn't—that an activity that had once sustained me was now something I needed to let go for my own health and for both our sanities. She told me, "John, it's time you stop playing basketball." At once, the statement made my heart sink and immediately felt right. It was time to let go. I haven't played a day of basketball since (other than shooting casually with my young son). But I found other hobbies and fitness activities to take its place, and my life became healthier and more meaningful as a result.

Letting go of things that have given us purpose is hard. Sure, for some, putting down the basketball or saying goodbye to another hobby might be relatively easy. But leaving a job or a bad relationship behind can be much more challenging. Once we've dedicated time and effort to something, it's difficult to leave it behind. If you're a lawyer who has tired of law, for example, how do you justify leaving the profession for which you dedicated seven years of higher education and hundreds of thousands of dollars? If you're a senior marketer, how do you justify trading decades of experience to start over in something new? If you've lived in a city long enough to develop friends and a routine, how do you uproot yourself and find something new?

Often we allow our present and future to be determined by our past commitments. We allow momentum, experience, and risk aversion to wed us inexorably to our path. But there are ways to offset the stress of letting go.

Carefully diagnose your feelings

First, understand why you feel the need to let something go in enough detail to determine if wholesale abandonment is really justified or if you simply need to change elements of the experience while keeping its core.

For instance, a friend of mine recently grew tired of his job in investments and considered leaving the profession entirely. But what he'd really grown tired of was working in a large, publicly traded corporation where politics were prized above performance. What he really needed was to stay in his profession but join a smaller firm where his leadership and ownership could mean more to the success of the organization and where the culture was a better fit.

If you're a lawyer tired of law, maybe you *should* be a baker or business owner—or maybe you should explore practicing a different type of law for different ends under different circumstances. Careful reflection on what you're leaving and why can prevent you from hastily abandoning something entirely without proper consideration for whether you're abandoning the right thing for the right reasons.

Realistically evaluate the trade-offs

Many people encourage you to "follow your passions" almost flippantly, but if you do decide to make a change, the first step is thinking realistically about what your new path will look like. If you're an investment banker who would like to work in a nonprofit, for example, you should take a hard look at what that change will mean practically for your future—a decline in financial rewards, the need to learn new leadership lessons and to potentially start over, and the details of the new job that will continue once your initial optimism has faded. It serves no one for you to leave a job, a community, or a friendship without considering what you are leaving them for in realistic terms. And you should rarely make a leap without knowing where you will land.

Look to the future—and embrace some risk

Once you've considered the practical realities of your choice to move, change professions, abandon a hobby, or exit a relationship, you may decide it's worth taking a risk. I was recently speaking with a peer in her early forties who was asking, "How can I leave something I've worked at for 20 years?" My encouragement to her was to ask instead, "Is this the thing to which I want to dedicate my next 20 years?" Your past is past. Sometimes things that gave you purpose no longer do. Allowing your past to determine your present and future can rob you of your life's potential. And no one wants to dedicate their next 20 years to something joyless or purposeless just because it was central to their last 20 years.

One of my favorite contemporary writers is Amor Towles. Towles was a successful finance executive from 1991 to 2012, but after the success of his first novel, *Rules of Civility*, he quit banking to pursue a career as a novelist. He's since published *Eve in Hollywood* and *A Gentleman in Moscow*. I'm sure leaving his career after the successful publication of one novel was not without risk. I'm sure it involved throwing away the things he'd learned over a 21-year career. But perhaps, for Towles, it was simply time to move on from one good thing to another—and his boldness in doing so introduced great literature to the world. Recent studies even indicate that risk-takers are happier with their lives.[1] Sometimes, after careful consideration, it's time to take a risk and make a change.

It's hard to navigate the new without pruning the old. Don't let your loyalty to the past unilaterally set your course for the future. When you know something has lost purpose for you and you've weighed the realistic consequences of letting go, have the confidence to make a change. One of life's best features is its variety and changeability. Learn to embrace both what's permanent for you and your shifting sources of meaning and to use transitions and stagnation alike to re-craft the purpose in your life.

Embracing change worksheet

What are three to five areas you consider permanent sources of purpose in your life? How can you invest more in them?

Source of purpose	Ways to invest

Are you in a transition? What's the nature of that transition, and what are the opportunities to mine new sources of meaning?

Are you feeling stagnant in any area of your life? Why?

What are some ways in which you can begin to mine and make new meaning in that area of your life?

Is there anything in your life that you may need to let go? What can you do instead to feel a sense of purpose?

NOTE

1. Jennifer Warner, "Are Risk Takers Happier?," WebMd, September 19, 2005, https://www.webmd.com/balance/news/20050919/are-risk-takers-happier.

SECTION THREE

Building Your Purpose

CHAPTER 7

Craft Your Work

By his own account, Eric Crouch was a poor student. Heading into college, he was aimless and unmotivated, ultimately dropping out with a 1.7 GPA to pursue his passion, photography. He and his brother, who also struggled at school, had never had much luck with their teachers, and so he didn't value classroom education. Then he got engaged, and the woman he wanted to marry insisted he get a degree, so he re-enrolled in college.

He quickly discovered a passion for education—a desire to help kids like him who had never had someone to guide them in school. He worked hard, raised his GPA, and ultimately graduated with a BA in education. Upon graduating, he landed a first-grade teaching spot at Double Churches Elementary, a public school in Columbus, Georgia. From the beginning, he let the school leaders at Double Churches know he was unlikely to teach like others and he might break some rules, but he'd always dedicate himself fully to his kids. And that's just what he does.

Eric's philosophy is that kids—even as young as first grade—need to take ownership for their own education, and that reaching each student requires understanding them personally and allowing them to a jointly create an individualized learning plan that will facilitate their success:

> *I would spend the first three weeks in the classroom just getting to know my kids. Playing games, interacting with them, learning how they interact with others. And then I thought, well, if I can teach them how they learn best, then I can get them on their own track to being independent and then we can create an autonomous classroom. . . .*
>
> *[I] learned very quickly that I don't write well sitting at a desk, and I don't type well sitting at a desk. I like to sit on the floor, and I like my computer to be elevated . . . and so I thought, if this is me, then what about my kids? What are my kids coming to school thinking they're not good at because they haven't been given an opportunity to feel it in a different way?*

Eric writes annual lesson plans and goals but mostly ignores them. Each day he has a yellow legal pad with goals on it for the day, and he loves constantly changing things up. "I get bored easily," he tells me with a laugh. Rather than creating a grading rubric, he asks students to cocreate it with him one-on-one and then jointly agree to accountability to the standard. If a student is gifted, she can zoom ahead. If she is struggling, Eric will find creative ways to bring the subject to life.

Recently, his fifth-grade students needed to think about math differently, so Eric formed a partnership with a school in Kenya. The agreement was his students would teach their African counterparts math through online videos, and their counterparts would teach them Swahili. "I thought, this would be a great opportunity for these kids to really learn something unique," he tells me, "but also to showcase what they do know and have mastered in mathematics and build some confidence as we're trying to build on top of those mathematic principles." They also learned a foreign language, social studies, and ultimately business and economics—starting a social enterprise in the classroom to support their sister school, resulting in a new well and community garden for that school.

A different cohort worked with Eric and a film crew to photograph and video the aftereffects of Hurricane Michael that was used to raise $2 million to buy school supplies for those devastated by the storm. What's the subject? Take your pick—social studies, art, economics, history, government.

He's convinced school leadership to let him teach his students every subject now, rather than rotating them, so these kinds of integrative lessons can have real impact and focus. And his test scores and popularity with students buy him the freedom to do so. At night, Eric leaves on time and gets to play with his two kids, hang out with his wife, and engage in his hobbies. He doesn't bring work or grading home since everything happens in the classroom, and that keeps him energized each day. "I'm coming in at 100%," he says, "going hey man, let's go do a project. Let's go work in the community. Let's go do something else. Because I'm getting to do other things that I love during the workweek."

How's all this working? Eric's test scores are great. His students love him. He's won the National Milken Educator Award, a GTP Top 50 Teacher in the World Award, a Harvard PZ Fellowship, and he's been asked to serve on the state superintendent's Teacher Advisory Council. Not bad for a kid who was never very good at school.

The Art of Job Crafting

Yale Professor Amy Wrzesniewski once did an in-depth study of hospital custodial staff to determine what helped certain members of the team excel. Wrzesniewski, an organizational psychologist, uncovered a practice among the happiest and most effective custodians she (and others) have termed "job crafting."[1] These custodial workers, focused intensely on serving patients, would "[create] the work they wanted to do out of the work they'd been assigned—work they found meaningful and worthwhile." One would rearrange artwork in rooms to stimulate comatose patients' brains; others devoted time to learning about the chemicals they used for cleaning rooms and figuring out which were least likely to irritate patients' conditions. They were pursuing excellence in service to others and would adapt their jobs to suit that purpose. They enhanced their assigned work to be meaningful to themselves and to those they serve.

TABLE 7-1

Craft your work

Opportunity to craft	What it looks like
Understand what gives you meaning, and attempt to shift your responsibilities	Tracking the types of activities that give you purpose and enjoyment throughout your week so you have an understanding of what best suits you, and then reflecting on those things and trying to emphasize them in your work.
Take on new tasks that are meaningful	Structuring time in your workweek to take on new tasks or activities that are meaningful and enjoyable to you—whether directly relevant to your job or in service of the broader organization.
Do the same job in a different way	Understanding what you need to achieve in your job and mapping your key tasks against it—then pruning the tasks that are not important and finding ways to make your essential tasks more meaningful.

In their own sphere, they did precisely what Eric Crouch does in his classroom.

Wrzesniewski and her frequent coauthors Justin Berg and Jane Dutton lay out three core elements of job crafting in their research.[2] They are:

1. **Tasks:** The specific actions you take each day as part of your work.

2. **Relationships:** Your relationships with others at work.

3. **Perceptions:** The way you think about your work.

In this chapter, we'll zero in on "task crafting"—pragmatic ways in which you can tweak the nature of your daily work to make it more meaningful, fulfilling, and even more effective. Task crafting involves taking the day-to-day activities and either reinventing them to be more meaningful or subtly shifting some responsibilities to spend more time on those that are most purposeful to you and less time on those that aren't. It's the middle manager, for example, deciding to delegate more project management to their core team while spending more time on coaching people through those activities. Or it's the employee in purchasing taking a manual process for vendor management and exploring her interest in technology by innovating that process through a new software platform.

Making practical changes to the work you do every day, in conjunction with making work a craft (which is discussed in the next chapter) can revitalize your professional life.

Identify what gives you meaning

Perhaps the best book I've read on constructing a career is *Designing Your Life*, by Bill Burnett and Dave Evans. The book helps readers apply design thinking (the kind the authors employed at places like Apple and Electronic Arts) to their lives—consciously crafting a more fulfilling existence. In it, the authors have a variety of exercises including what they call a "good time journal," a simple one-page sheet used to track the energy and engagement you feel from activities throughout the day.

Doing the exercise daily for a few weeks offers deep insight into which activities excite and engage you and which activities drain you—from intense negotiations to team meetings and periods of prolonged heads-down work. When I completed the exercise, for example, I noted spikes in my energy and engagement when I was involved in coaching and talent development, sales, or negotiations. But I noticed both lagged in process meetings. Somewhere in the middle were feedback discussions and employee reviews, which I found engaging but drained my energy. It's an exercise that can help almost anyone learn more about themselves. I discovered that I often took particularly arduous activities on myself in order to spare my team, but I had probably overcorrected in doing so and risked burnout. One outcome of the exercise was that I personally redesigned my responsibilities so that I could spend more time on the things that offered me energy and engagement each day, thoughtfully shifting some of the other activities to others (and learning that some people actually enjoyed those other activities in the process).

A similar exercise can be used for purpose. Instead of tracking your energy and engagement, track purpose and enjoyment, as you did in the two-by-two introduced in chapter 2. Each day, note the major activities you're engaged in and rate them on the meaning and joy you feel from them. Think of it as a balance journal. Table 7-2 shows an example for Krista, a partner at an accounting firm. Keeping the journal may help her spot the areas of her life in which it's most difficult to find purpose and joy—working to either recraft or eliminate those things—while simultaneously identifying areas in which she can invest more deeply that offer her great meaning and joy.

Keep the balance journal for a week. Which tasks are fun but meaningless? Keeping up with my Netflix

TABLE 7-2

Krista's balance journal

Activity	Purpose (1=low, 5=high)	Enjoyment (1=low, 5=high)
Get kids ready in the morning	4. Great to start the day connecting with them	3. It's always a little chaotic, and I have to wake up early
All-company morning meeting	2. Not very relevant to my work today	2. Good to hear from others but feels like an obligation
Coffee with mentee	5. Really feels like we are making progress and she is growing	5. She has such a great personality and is a good listener
Meeting to pitch client	5. This is what I'm good at and I know it pays off for the firm	5. Really engaging group, and I wowed them
Review compliance logs for team	2. Someone has to do this, but a lot seems irrelevant or like someone else could do it	1. Ugh
Work block to review client audit	4. This is what we do and it's our core client service	3. Becoming more of a chore
Client meeting regarding recent audit	4. Direct client service. Good finished product	5. Clients were receptive and grateful. I liked presenting
Meeting with managing partner and team	2. Seemed aimless, more for my benefit	3. Nice to get face time but was stressful and accomplished little
Review for underperforming associate	5. He needed the coaching and needs to prepare if an exit comes	3. Tough. I know it's important, but it's draining

queue makes the list for me. Which tasks are incredibly meaningful but hard? Which are both fun and meaningful? And which are neither? Once you know how you're spending your time, try to create more time for the purposeful and fun tasks and find ways to spend less time on the meaningless ones. Eric Crouch may never be a school leader because he's slow on email and doesn't place a high value on consistent faculty meeting attendance. But he loves creativity and one-on-one interactions with kids. And you know what? He's found a way to do more of what he loves while radically changing the lives of kids.

Sometimes it's not as hard to shift responsibilities and craft a more fulfilling schedule as you think. Often teams are populated with complementary people. Some love process and checklists, others love "blue sky" thinking and strategy. Some love public speaking and group brainstorming, while others love writing and working independently. Once you have a better understanding of what you find purposeful and enjoyable, think about your team. Are there responsibilities you might swap with a teammate that could make both your lives better—handing off running staff meetings, for example, but taking on recruitment? If your manager is receptive, it's also possible for you to engage them in the activity. Speak to them about what you've learned from this exercise, and ask if there are ways they can help you prioritize the activities that are best for you over time and delegate others to fellow team members.

Take on new tasks that are meaningful

One of the smartest colleagues I've had was a young man on a team I managed whose primary job was "strategy"—to help us think through business problems and their solutions in new and impactful ways. He had an interest, however, in two areas only tangentially related to his work—startups and data science. So, he and I worked out an agreement that he could spend 10%–20% of his time on these passion projects, by joining a task force working on community startups and enrolling in a data science course part-time. It was extra work for him and less time he could dedicate to our core initiatives, but these projects energized him and made work more meaningful with him (and it kept him more committed to our team and the firm).

Many good managers are open to people pursuing passion projects that are only tangentially related to their core work or are not related at all. It usually is a compromise, more work for the person who picks up the new activity and less work for the team they support. But the greater energy and purpose it creates can be a win for everyone. Are there affinity groups in your organization—a women's network, for example—that you could help lead and give you meaning? Is there a passion project you could work on for another department that would offer you purpose and even broaden your career prospects? Is there a class you could enroll in that would enhance your sense of purpose while providing you with new skills?

Look at the opportunities around you, and carefully consider each one. Don't overdo it or take on too much at once. Many people are already overburdened with work. Often the same people get tapped to support multiple groups, and sometimes managers are not open to reducing workload to accommodate new tasks. Exercise your judgment about what you can do while retaining real balance in your life and what the organization will find acceptable. If you can make the time commitments work, prevent your own burnout, and persuade your team's leadership of the value of your activities—passion projects can be a real source of meaning. And often, where the activity is genuinely valuable to your organization as well as to you it will display real initiative and entrepreneurship to those around you.

Do the same job in a different way

When Eric and his students got bored with conventional lessons, they learned Swahili, started businesses, and created a film and photography program that lifted up thousands of other students. Eric reaches the same (or better) outcomes as other teachers, but he's found a way to do that job and to achieve those outcomes that is radically different than the way most teachers operate. Such an unconventional approach works for him. And his unique insight is that the method also works for students, who are energized and achieve real ownership by creating lesson plans that work for them. This is the same technique employed by Wrzesniewski's janitors, who would tweak the way they accomplished their core tasks in ways that made them more meaningful and effective. You can do the same in your own role.

I worked with a newly minted MBA, for example, who grew tired of some of the more repetitive elements of our reporting function—cleansing data, manually manipulating it, and creating charts. But she loved technology and advanced analytics. So she asked to take on a midterm project in which we'd slim down reports for a period of time so that she could build a more sophisticated and automatic way of processing the data using new technology and analytical method. It was fantastic—a win for us as a team and for her sense of purpose. Could you do the same?

Try the following activity:

1. Draw three columns. Write down the 10–20 core elements of your job in the center column. Similarly write down the 5–10 key outcomes you need to achieve in your job in the third column.

2. See where the core elements of your job and key outcomes connect, and draw lines between them. You may not be able to draw neat lines between all of them—some outcomes require multiple tasks, and some tasks lead to multiple outcomes.

3. Identify opportunities to streamline elements. Strike out any tasks with no real outcomes. Now circle the tasks you find most cumbersome, meaningless, or uninspiring.

4. Finally, brainstorm replacement tasks. How could you replace the meaningless tasks with something more meaningful while achieving the same impact? Jot down these ideas in the first column.

Table 7-3 shows an example of this as it may have looked for one of my old colleagues, whom we'll call Carla, in sales support.

Now complete yours and reflect on it. Are there creative way to reshape your work that could make it

TABLE 7-3

Carla's task reinvention worksheet

Task reinvention	Current tasks	Key work outcomes
• Build out tech platform to automate import, analysis, presentation • More time on analysis	• Importing and cleaning data from systems • Running Excel analysis • Filling in PPT presentation • Presenting to management	• Quarterly management reports to drive sales
• Upgrade features to include mobile and voice • Create and conduct training for sales	• Get meeting notes from sales and enter • Survey sales for client updates and enter	• Keep salesforce updated with client notes
• Create strategy for high-probability buyers • Access data source for client type • Feed to sales and workshop	• Ask sales team for prospects • Classify each • Ask for updates	• Create prospect list for new product sales
• Cut task	• ~~Data entry for product report~~	• Product report No one reads!

more meaningful and as or more impactful at the same time? Once you have these ideas written down, discuss them with your boss or with members of your team who might be affected. Be ready to articulate how these changes will benefit them while also increasing your engagement. Use the following tips for how to propose your changes:

1. **Make them proactive and solutions-oriented.** Many managers are accustomed to hearing problems all day but not getting proposed solutions. If you come with a plan, they are more likely to listen.

2. **Ensure they meet the needs of the company and team.** A good manager wants to keep her team engaged while also achieving the goals of the team and company. If your plan neglects the core purpose of your job or doesn't achieve the necessary outcomes of the team, it won't be accepted. Draft a plan that is neutral or better for the team.

3. **Don't unduly burden your colleagues.** It would be nice to get rid of all the things we don't like at work and keep all the things we do. And, indeed, most jobs can be dramatically redrafted with a little creativity. But if your plan simply shifts the most difficult items to other team members, it's not reasonable.

4. **Prove the case first (if you can).** Wrzesniewski's janitors didn't present plans to managers. They simply started doing their jobs better. Some of the reinvention you imagine you can simply begin to do—testing its efficacy—and communicate once your case is proved. This won't work all the

time—on critical processes for example, or where some spending is involved. But it often will.

When presented this way, many managers will not only engage and be open to change but appreciate the reflection and entrepreneurship. You might not get everything you want, and you may even hear a "no." If that happens, try not to be too frustrated or discouraged. Sometimes managers have good reasons to decline your proposal. They might need to balance the needs and interests of various constituents, they may have context you don't, or they may simply disagree with the approach. If your boss does turn you down, take some time to regroup and make a new plan of action. (The sidebar "What to Do If Your Boss Says 'No'" offers tips on how to continue the discussion and offer an alternate proposal.)

But for many people, job or task crafting is a great path toward reinvigorating your work and making it more meaningful and enjoyable. Who knows—by reinventing your own work, you may even inspire others to do the same, improving the culture around you.

WHAT TO DO IF YOUR BOSS SAYS "NO"

Sometimes when we attempt to craft our jobs, we hear a "no." After a lot of hard work, thought, and hopefulness for the future, having someone turn down our ideas can come as a shock. So, what do you do when your boss says no to your thoughtful task crafting? Here are a few suggestions:

WHAT TO DO IF YOUR BOSS SAYS "NO"

- ***Approach the conversation with curiosity.*** Before you even enter the room to ask about enacting a change, make sure your mindset is right. You are one person on a team. Your boss has their own concerns. Approach the conversation with empathy and a genuine desire to discuss the proposal and understand the other person's concerns.

- ***Ask good questions.*** When you hear a no, it can be tempting to get defensive. That's almost never the right approach. Instead, defuse the situation and learn more by asking thoughtful questions. Try to understand not just what the other person is saying but why they are saying it—their root concerns. If you can address those, it's possible there's still room for a good outcome.

- ***Ask for time to process.*** Put a pause on the conversation, so you can digest what you've heard. This could be as simple as saying something like, "I really appreciate the feedback and you've given me a lot to process. Would you mind if I think through this for a few days and come back to you with a few thoughts?" This will offer you time to gain perspective, understand the other person's concerns, and reformulate your ask.

- ***Take a day or two to reflect.*** Once you've asked for time, take it. Take 24 hours away from your proposal to relax and get distance. Especially if you're feeling frustration, cooling off for a day can help you think more rationally and empathetically. Then give yourself a day or two to consider the problem anew. Often, it's also helpful to reflect with a third-party friend or colleague who can help you see things in a new light.

- ***Adapt your proposal.*** After reflecting, if you still see value in a change, try to meaningfully address the other person's concerns and reposition the ask. Present it to them by leading with what you heard the last time and how you addressed it. This has the double benefit of making that person feel understood and generating initial agreement.
- ***Don't let the perfect be the enemy of the good.*** Your plan may be perfect to you, but if you can't get it all, it may be enough to get some of it. Don't let the pursuit of perfection rob you of a meaningful and fulfilling path forward.

If, after all your careful thought your boss still does not budge, reflect on how important these changes are to you. Are there other areas of purpose in your life on which you might focus? Are there other opportunities to craft your work? Only after careful consideration of these questions should you consider larger changes.

NOTES

1. Justin M. Berg, Jane E. Dutton, and Amy Wrzesniewski, "What Is Job Crafting and Why Does It Matter?," Ross School of Business, http://positiveorgs.bus.umich.edu/wp-content/uploads/What-is-Job-Crafting-and-Why-Does-it-Matter1.pdf.

2. Amy Wrzesniewski, Justin M. Berg, and Jane E. Dutton, "Managing Yourself: Turn the Job You Have into the Job You Want," *Harvard Business Review*, June 2010, https://hbr.org/2010/06/managing-yourself-turn-the-job-you-have-into-the-job-you-want.

CHAPTER 8

Make Work a Craft

Luke Pontifell, founder of Thornwillow Press, traces his love of craft to his childhood in a restored eighteenth-century farmhouse in western Massachusetts. From the aged planks and preserved character of his home he learned a reverence for the power of physical things. He loves the history of such places. His mother was a sculptor and his father a writer and advertising executive. And they further taught him creativity and the importance of working with his hands.

Luke discovered the craft that would dominate his life—letterpress printing, papermaking, and book binding—while a student at Harvard College. He took a class on letterpress at the Center for Book Arts in New York City and fell in love. As he learned the art, he wrote famous authors and garnered permission to do special letterpress runs of their books or essays. That first experience peaked when German Chancellor Helmut Kohl spoke at his Harvard graduation in 1990. In that speech,

Kohl laid out his plan for German reunification and the future of Europe. Luke got Chancellor Kohl's permission to do an exclusive, limited letterpress edition of his remarks.

After graduation, he joined Mont Blanc, and found himself working out of Germany and visiting a paper mill in the Czech Republic. The owners of the mill told him he couldn't buy paper, but he could buy the mill. Mont Blanc agreed to be his first customer. And in a stroke of fate, Luke became the world's largest manufacturer of handmade paper—only to have the factory stolen from him during the tumult of the post-Soviet era. "We lost everything," Luke says. "Every penny I had invested, I lost. But we sold our home to scrape it all together and started over."

He and his wife moved back to New York and decided to start a comprehensive business in papermaking and letterpress in the cheapest place they could find convenient to New York City—Newburgh, New York. People told them it would be impossible.

> *[When we moved to Newburgh], the one thing that we were told by everyone is there's no way you could do this in America. That you'll never find the craftspeople with . . . generations of skill. . . . And in some ways that advice was right. In other ways we've made it our mission to prove it wrong. And we found very quickly we had to get into the business of teaching and perpetuating these crafts.*

With Thornwillow, Luke has two core businesses, the business of making beautiful handmade objects—stationery, business cards, special limited-run letterpress editions of great books—and the business of teaching others his craft. Speaking to him you hear his deep passion for making things that last, things that can matter, things that have, in his words, "soul."

> *An object can have a soul when . . . it's integral to the artistic experience, when it forms a bond between the creator, the author, the composer, and . . . the people on the receiving end. [A]lso when that object becomes like a memorial . . . when it becomes part of your identity.*

Luke and his colleagues at Thornwillow have rediscovered that in the age of mass production and disposable items, attention to beauty, detail, trade, and craft can transform the ordinary to the extraordinary. They've discovered how craft itself can create meaning.

Craft in a Disposable Age

Have you ever thought about how the very act of pouring yourself into something can give it soul? Until I spoke to Luke, I'd never considered it in those terms. Yet now, I can't escape the thought that that's exactly what I respect when I see a job well done. It's easy to see, of course, in grand masterpieces—the *Mona Lisa*, the pyramids at Giza, Stonehenge, or *Paradise Lost*. But in smaller ways, we can all experience the same types of appreciation and meaning in our daily lives—the barista who prepares the perfect cup of coffee or the colleague whose PowerPoint presentations are both functional and beautiful. And most of us have had the transformative experience of really disciplining ourselves to be great at something at

TABLE 8-1

Make work a craft

Method	What it looks like
Identify the opportunities for craft in your work	Reflecting on your core work activities and looking for areas in which you could develop real mastery and craft, then communicating those goals to others who can keep you accountable and celebrate your victories with you.
Pursue an avocation that allows for craft	Doubling down on an existing hobby where you can devote conscious effort to increased mastery or finding a new hobby you'd like to master—whether running, knitting, painting, writing, or any of a host of other activities.
Compete	Taking those avocations where you are developing mastery to the next level by finding ways to compete or showcase your work—allowing others to see it, measuring your own work against that of others, and measuring your current performance against your own performances in the past.
Learn to see and appreciate the craft of others	Learning to see and appreciate the craft of others—both those you know personally and those you do not; really taking time to study the work of someone who does something extraordinarily well both to appreciate it and to learn from it.

work—treating it with the same perfection Luke Pontifell treats each of his editions of *The Great Gatsby* or *Pride and Prejudice*. That act of perfecting something, pushing the bounds of human accomplishment, creates meaning.

As opposed to the "task crafting" we learned in the last chapter, making something a craft means deeply investing yourself in the perfection of the activity, becoming the best you can be at it. Craft often results in what we previously learned psychologist Mihaly Csikszentmihalyi called "flow," a mental state in which you are totally immersed in your work and the world seems to melt away. That state often leads to an enhanced sense of purpose.

Where do you have a sense of craft in your life? If we turn back to our LABORS framework, craft can manifest in either avocations (our hobbies or attempts at self-improvement) or occupation. It often results in beauty—whether the beauty of a well-made shoe to a cobbler or an elegant formula for a mathematician or financial analyst. It's often a work done in service to others, out of love, or even as an expression of our religious and philosophical beliefs (hence the beauty of so many great religious structures around the world). Yet, many people become so trapped in the doldrums of life they forget the thrill and satisfaction of a job well done, of the act of painstakingly learning a craft and creating works of art from even the simplest of tasks.

Does this sound familiar to you? Have you lost a sense of craft at work? Are you lacking something that allows you to be a creator and get meaning from the discipline of a job perfectly and lovingly executed?

If so, the good news is this is perhaps one of the easiest ways in which to make purpose. Restoring a sense of craft to your life and work is as easy as identifying the opportunities for growth in your profession, assuring you always have an avocation or hobby you can improve on, and learning to see and appreciate the skill of others. Here are a few ways to imbue your life with more craft.

Identify the opportunities for craft in your work

In my younger days as a business analyst at McKinsey, I found a satisfaction building Excel models. I'd never really used Excel until I graduated college, but once I started using it I was hooked. I loved to build incredibly complex models that were simple to use—to craft elegant little formulas and macros that made them interactive and accessible to anyone. I loved picking just the right fonts and colors to make them as visually appealing as they were accurate. I'd literally come home from work, have dinner, and leap into model building for hours, often losing track of time and finding myself up at two or three in the morning.

Maybe Excel models aren't quite as inspiring as beautiful hand-bound books, a perfectly orchestrated symphony, or even a well-brewed cup of coffee. But to me, they were an opportunity for craft, to transform what could have been mechanical exercises into works of art. And I suspect there are millions of people out there who feel the same—who see a potential to create art where others may only see a task.

Write out five activities that require skill and attention to detail at work. Perhaps you'd identify crafting poetic legal briefings, designing a flawless website, building an elegant pitch deck for your startup, or carefully learning the names and interests of the colleagues with whom you work. The activities don't have to be revolutionary—they need only be important to you and offer the opportunity for you to build your skill level over time. Set specific, measurable goals for yourself (for example, "I will know the names of each colleague on my floor in 30 days") or share your aspirations with others (including your manager) where the activity is more subjective—such as an outstanding PowerPoint or user-friendly Excel model. Sharing your goals with others—team members, colleagues, or peers—commits you to these goals and allows you to engage your partners in your journey of self-improvement and mastery. I would often do this as a manager, letting my team know projects I was working on and asking them to provide feedback on my progress. It also modeled the kind of craft I was looking for from them. What are the areas in which you can practice craft, and who can you engage to celebrate with you and hold you accountable?

Pursue a hobby that allows for craft

I had a work colleague who had a remarkable Etsy store. She made finely crafted sculptures from nature—eagles, horses, and antelope, among other things. She was never going to be a professional sculptor, in the sense of pursuing it as a career rather than an avocation. It would never pay the bills, and she was happy in her job. Nevertheless, she was passionate about sculpting, spending untold hours improving her craft, bringing greater beauty to the world one small piece at a time.

The fact that this hobby would never be her career did nothing to diminish the purpose and enjoyment she found in her art. I've found similar meaning in the repetition and perfection-seeking of multiple avocations that have varied through my life—writing, humor, public speaking, or running. And I bet you have, too, whether that particular pursuit was Toastmasters, CrossFit, or Fortnite.

Obviously, some avocations are more edifying than others. Winston Churchill, for example, found solace and purpose in painting at the heights of his struggles with depression (his "black dog") and the World War. He wrote a book about the power of this hobby in his life, *Painting as a Pastime*. It has inspired countless others to adopt the hobby, including U.S. President George W. Bush, who processed some of the most important challenges he's faced through art. Warren Buffett plays ukulele, Nick Offerman does woodworking, Leslie Mann unicycles, and Susan Sarandon is a Ping-Pong enthusiast. Some people take up their own health and well-being as an avocation, using meditation to sharpen their minds and relieve anxiety or training in a sport to improve their physical health.

What are your hobbies? In chapter 5 we emphasized their importance. Here, we should examine their craft. As with your occupation, sit and write down opportunities for craft in one or two of your most important avocations. Begin to set your own improvement goals and hold yourself accountable to those goals—perhaps incorporating feedback from friends or a significant other or by competing (as in the next section). In exercise, this is easy. Committing to set personal bests on your Peloton each month, for example, or improving your 5K time by 5% per month is a quantifiable goal. In other areas—from cooking to music—you may need more subjective measures or the feedback of a community through performance of competition. Find a buddy to do the activity with you, encourage you, or hold you accountable to pursuing your craft.

Turning a hobby into an opportunity for craft can be the difference between a mindless pursuit and the pursuit of mindfulness and meaning.

Find opportunities to compete

There's a reason millions of people sign up for road races each year—5Ks, 10Ks, marathons—even though they know they'll be, at best, average in their fields. There's a reason "gamification" is such a buzzword in business. And there's a reason your sixth grader preps for spelling and geography bees, and almost every kid loves participating in annual field days at school.

Many of us are wired for competition. We find the process of competing—not just winning but competing itself—edifying. Participating in a competition allows you to make your skills public and weigh them against the talents of others. It incentivizes you to focus and improve and can create meaningful moments both when you gain an edge over the competition and when you fail but stand back up and try again.

Once you've identified opportunities for craft in your work and avocations that allow for craft, find ways to compete: chili cook-offs, CrossFit competitions, judo matches, dog shows, photography competitions, or work hackathons can all provide an outlet to not only focus deeply on skill building but to measure your progress against that of others and put yourself to the test. Some people fear competition, but healthy competition in multiple areas of your life can be edifying and lead to real focus on craft in all you do. The purpose of competition is winning. But the key to healthy competition is realizing the meaning in simply committing to improvement and progress in the things we love.

You've listed tasks at work and avocations that you can craft earlier in this chapter. Now how can you compete? Competition can be as grand as entering the Boston Marathon or as simple as finding five friends to text the number of steps you've taken that day. At work, it can be entering a hackathon as a computer programmer or coming up with goals as a team that everyone can pursue as a friendly game over the course of a week or month.

If the idea of competing publicly is just not your thing, or if the craft you are pursuing doesn't lend itself to formal competition, find ways to compete with yourself. Track your personal bests at weightlifting and commit to improving them. Time your performance of a task at work and watch it shorten as you become proficient. Monitor your students' test scores and commit, internally, to incremental improvement for your classes each year. It can still be worthwhile to compete with others, but sometimes it is healthiest and easiest to simply compete with one's past self.

Appreciate the craft of others

Sportswriter Bill Simmons once wrote a remarkable little article titled "God Loves Cleveland." The article, published on Grantland.com, is focused on LeBron James's 2014 decision to leave Miami and return to his hometown team in Ohio. But my favorite passages from the piece are from an aside Simmons writes on the poetry and intensity of watching Michael Jordan play basketball. In part, he writes:

> *I watched Jordan play in person, many times, at various stages of his career. My favorite version was post-baseball MJ—a little humbled, a little wiser, still kicking everyone's collective rear end—when the Bulls occasionally rolled through Boston and eviscerated the carcass of Celtic Pride. One particular night, we turned on the locals and started cheering what we were watching. It didn't happen because we were selling out, but because we had witnessed a special kind of greatness during the Bird Era. We knew what it meant. We knew how fragile it was. We missed seeing it. Watching those Bulls was like catching up with an old friend.*

Jordan was the greatest basketball player of all time—perhaps the greatest athlete of all time. Millions of people around the world grew up admiring him—people of all races and creeds, in every country, even those who cared nothing for basketball. Because something in us is drawn to greatness, to seeing a thing performed in ways that defy human limitation and exhibit otherworldly craft. We love to watch Serena Williams fire a serve, Dustin Johnson hit a perfect drive, Bruce Springsteen bring down the house with a live performance, or Maya Angelou read poetry. And those who know a craft appreciate its perfection even more.

Like anything, we can train ourselves to appreciate a craft more. The late Clayton Christensen, one of the most remarkable minds in the history of business, recounted a story once about his first year as a student at Harvard Business School. He would sit quietly in the back of class and keep a journal of the best questions his classmates had asked that day. At home he'd reflect on that journal, marveling at the insight of a great question and, step-by-step, training his own mind to formulate them.

You're surrounded by extraordinarily talented people every day. Reflecting on some of those people, how they achieve their attention to craft, and the impact that has on them and others can deepen your sense of appreciation and gratitude while also encouraging you on your journey of self-improvement. Ask yourself:

1. Who are five people in my life who display extraordinary craft in something that they do?
2. What do they do, and what makes it so extraordinary?
3. What practice or talent must it take to achieve that craft?
4. What sacrifices have they made?
5. What can I learn from it?

For example, I once had an executive assistant who treated her job with extraordinary craft. She was methodical about her basic responsibilities, often helping me to better manage my schedule in ways I didn't even know I needed—scheduling travel time between meetings, color coding my calendar, blocking out dedicated work time, and helping me think through my meeting rhythm with my team and even consistent places to have meetings. Then, because she was so incredibly efficient, she became our team's de facto head of communications and client experience—leading projects and helping us improve communications. On top of all this, she did each of these things with a remarkable attitude and sense of positivity. I was extraordinarily impressed by her dedication to constantly improving her craft, and I learned a great deal from her.

Careful appreciation of others can rewire our brains—teaching us to look for the best in others, to appreciate the sacrifice and work of others, and to see more meaning in our own pursuit of craft.

A Call to Craft

There are enumerable opportunities for craft in your work and life. And the fulfillment and meaning you can get from becoming the best you can be—from perfecting something step by step—can be deeply rewarding. It can also inspire others to see their own lives differently and discern the opportunities they have to generate flow and a real sense of accomplishment. What are your opportunities to practice craft today and to celebrate it in the lives of others?

CHAPTER 9

Connect Your Work to Service

Lisa Hallett met her future husband, John, when she was in kindergarten and John was in second grade. All the way through school, they knew of each other, but were separated by two years—an eternity to a kid. Then, when Lisa was 15, she and John ended up on the same church mission trip building homes in Mexico. One day after framing seven houses together, Lisa fell in love. "I came home from that trip," she told me, "and I told anybody who would listen that I was going to marry John Hallett and have his red-headed babies."

They began dating in college when John was a senior at West Point and Lisa at UC Santa Barbara. They enjoyed a whirlwind romance before John graduated West Point in June of 2001. Three months later, Lisa was in San Francisco and John was at training in Fort Benning, Georgia, when the Twin Towers fell. Lisa followed John to a base in Hawaii, and they got married on December 27, 2003, three weeks before John deployed to Iraq. He was gone the first 14 months of their marriage. She then moved with him to Georgia, to Louisiana, and finally to Washington state, where John assumed company command in 2008. They had two beautiful little boys along the way. And Lisa was nearly nine months pregnant with their third, a daughter, when John deployed to Afghanistan on July 11, 2009.

On August 25, John was killed in Southern Afghanistan. He was on a mercy mission to a village with a cholera outbreak when he was attacked. Back in Washington, Lisa was crushed by the news that the love of her life had given his life for his country. She was left to care for three young children, including a daughter who had never met her dad. "All those terrible things you've seen in movies had become my life," she told me. "And I thought, I am never going to be happy again."

She turned to running. On runs, she could cry without her young children seeing her hurt and scared. She started that first week with her friend Carrie. As more and more soldiers in her community died, she began to reach out to other women who, like her, were suffering. And one day a group of them got together—all spouses from John's company, the 1-17 Buffaloes. They donned their husbands' old training shirts, blue with a big buffalo head on them, and they started running together.

Running became Lisa's mission and a sacred space. It became a way to connect with and help others cope. And it became an occasion to remember those she and so many others had lost. When she and the other military spouses would meet, they'd speak the names of the fallen and place remembrance flags along their running routes. As her running groups grew and as she saw the impact it had on the people around her, she realized she needed to do something more.

In 2011, she and cofounder Erin O'Connor started a nonprofit memorial running organization: wear blue: run to remember. From its base in Washington state, the organization has expanded to 48 running communities around the United States, including six anchor communities that meet every Saturday at the same time and place, often with hundreds of people joining. At the beginning of each run they stand in a circle and call out the names of the people they are remembering. They also sponsor or partner with 14 races around the country, where they host a "memory mile"—one mile of the race where they plant flags and the photos of those who have died. Over one million athletes have run through these memory miles, and Lisa's organization has honored more than 1,500 fallen service members. They now also have a Gold Star Youth mentorship program, through which they pair children of fallen soldiers with service members who can run with and mentor them. Lisa's own kids participate. She tells me, "It gives them a community that empowers them but doesn't revictimize them. And that's what I want for them."

Lisa is a phenomenal mom to her three beautiful kids. She still loves John. She has a master's in education and has worked all over the field, as, in her words, an "education hustler." She's a Gold Star spouse. She's a nonprofit founder and executive director. She helps others in their lowest moments. She's a person of deep faith, profound patriotism, and remarkable resilience.

And, like John, she's committed to service. Out of the most painful moment of her life came her life's most meaningful work.

Making Service Central

The most purposeful people you'll meet know that meaning is derived not from amassing accolades but helping others. And you don't have to have suffered a personal tragedy like Lisa to cultivate an attitude of service in your life. Anyone can realize that the secret to a fulfilled, meaningful life isn't wealth or power or fame but the joy of investing one's talents and experiences on behalf of others.

Simply put, service is the act of working primarily for the benefit of others. In a *Time* magazine article titled "The Secret to Happiness Is Helping Others," philanthropy specialist Jenny Santi reviews some of the evidence that service is central to happiness and concludes: "Scientific research provides compelling data to support the anecdotal evidence that giving is a powerful pathway to personal growth and lasting happiness." Researchers at the University of Chicago and Northwestern University have run experiments demonstrating that giving gifts to others brings more lasting happiness than giving gifts to oneself.[1] And the Corporation for National and Community Service in the United States has published extensively on the positive impacts of service on life satisfaction and mental health.[2] Good works can even lengthen life expectancy.[3] Implicitly, we all know this.

TABLE 9-1

4C, 2P approach to service

	Who they are	What it looks like
Clients or customers	The primary people you serve in your work—the purpose of the organization you are in and the primary beneficiaries of the work that you do.	Cashiers taking extra time to cheer up customers; financial advisors who seek to truly understand the goals of their clients and to enable them; doctors who treat their patients empathetically as people rather than as cases.
Colleagues	The people you work with in an organization on a day-to-day basis.	Volunteering to be a mentor to colleagues who need it; putting in a few extra hours to help a colleague meet a deadline and taking no credit; sending flowers to a colleague who has experienced a death in the family.
Community	The community in which you live and work—your fellow citizens and the organizations that matter to your neighborhood, city, county, or state.	Encouraging the development of a charity matching program at your organization; taking your team out to volunteer at a soup kitchen; spending time outside of work investing in a tutoring organization for at-risk kids.
Capital	The shareholders of your company who benefit when you are successful—often pension funds, people saving for college, charitable institutions, and individuals like you.	Working conscientiously and as a fiduciary to ensure that those who depend on your organization for their retirements or college educations can meet their goals; understanding the ownership of your company so that you can better visualize the beneficiaries.
Partners	Vendors and service providers who view you as the client and who often depend on your patronage for their livelihoods.	Treating vendors, service providers, and JV partners with dignity and respect; holding them accountable while doing so humanely and with empathy; asking the consultant you're working with about their day and how they are feeling.
People you love	Those people outside of work who benefit from the work that you do.	Taking time to reflect on and acknowledge those who benefit from your hard work—parents in long-term care, kids in nursery school, a spouse pursuing a passion, friends you can support in their new ventures.

We've all felt it personally. But it can be hard to focus on in the midst of the trials, tribulations, and mundanities of daily life.

Connecting our day-to-day jobs—consciously and concretely—to those we're ultimately serving makes completing that work more purposeful. Finding opportunities for service, or to reconcile our existing work as service, can be the linchpin of purpose and happiness at work.

There are an almost infinite number of people or groups you could serve in the nearly infinite number of professions out there. And service looks different for an accountant, a lawyer, or a procurement specialist. Seeking to become more service-oriented is both a commitment to action and a change in mindset.

Frameworks are a helpful way in which to make sure you're at least hitting the basics. As you're considering how to best mine your own work for service, look in at least six areas. This is the "4C, 2P" approach to serving others, as shown in figure 9-1: Clients or customers, colleagues, capital, community, partners, and people you love.

Clients or customers

Bill George is a legendary executive. He held positions at the U.S. Department of Defense, Honeywell, and Litton before becoming chief operating officer and ultimately chief executive officer of Medtronic. During his tenure as CEO, he grew Medtronic from a $750 million heart device manufacturer to a $6.4 billion diversified medical device company. He retired from business in 2002,

FIGURE 9-1

The 4C, 2P approach to serving others

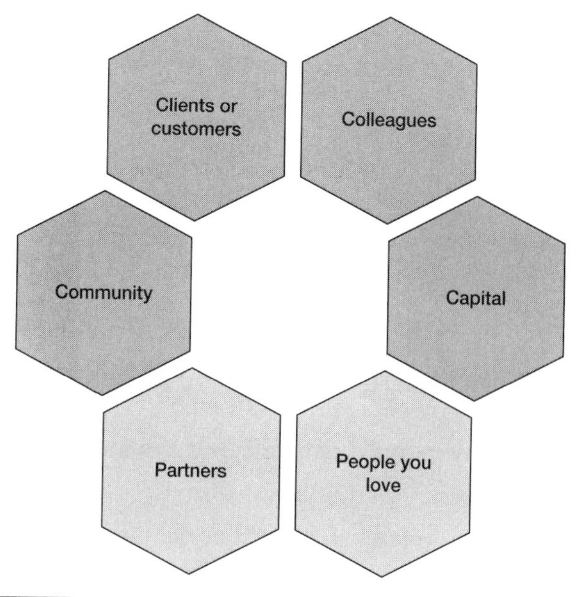

pursued an advanced degree, and started writing, teaching, and speaking about leadership. He's now the author of multiple books on "authentic leadership," a professor at Harvard Business School, a board member at some of the world's most important companies. He's also obsessed with purpose and meaning. If anyone could be fulfilled based on accomplishment alone, it's Bill. And yet he consistently sees his greatest moments in serving others and helping those who work with them connect their work to service—particularly service to clients and customers, the purest mission of any organization.

Bill once told a story about how he'd highlight both patients and employees at the Medtronic annual meeting. He'd invite a person whose life had been saved by a defibrillator, for example, to speak to his assembled colleagues and tell them how their work had saved his life. He'd highlight someone in the Medtronic quality control department and explain how her dedication and rigor were saving thousands of lives. He'd connect his colleagues directly to the people they served. These on-the-ground examples of the purpose of the organization and the meaning of the work its employees were doing day in and day out helped people in the company see their work not simply as a job but as a mission. Inevitably, that connection to those Medtronic's devices were saving offered meaning to Bill as well.

Now Bill's "clients" are his readers and students, and Bill takes his service to them as seriously as he did the life-or-death business of medical devices. He's funded a new building at Georgia Tech and has sponsored a fellowship at Harvard. He spends time with hundreds of students who pass through his classes or the programs he has crafted. He's active on social media, interacting with readers and former students, and, in his writing, he's dedicated to helping people find their own authentic leadership.

Who is the end client or customer of your organization? Is it a shopper in a grocery store with kids at home who need nutritious meals on a limited budget? Is it a student with raw talent who will be tragically overlooked without an astute teacher to guide her? Is it a hospital patient, frightened and clinging to life? Is it a couple in counseling who've brought you into their most important and painful moments? Or is it a caller having trouble with their mobile phone plan who just needs a helpful, pleasant person to talk to?

Taking time to reflect on and invest in the clients or customers of your work isn't only the foundation of any successful business, it's the fastest path to meaning. Ask yourself who your clients are, and then spend time thinking about their life empathetically—what their life away from you looks like, the pressures they feel, their fears and hopes. That deep empathy will allow you to better feel for and serve them. See the sidebar "Developing Empathy" for tips on how to grow this key skill.

Colleagues

When I was an early tenure consultant, I was on a particularly difficult assignment near Madison, Wisconsin. I woke up at 4 a.m. every Monday morning to catch a flight from Atlanta to Madison and usually got home late Thursday night. I stayed in a nice but nondescript hotel. I regularly worked 14–16 hour days while on site, and with the paucity of quick-serve restaurants in the area I ended up eating at Panera every day of the week. The content of our work—corporate strategy—was fascinating but the experience was exhausting. It could have been a very hard four months. But it was salvaged by a remarkable team. The four of us—men and women—were three different nationalities and a mix of personalities. But we each had a good sense of humor, a dedication to good work, and a willingness to invest in and serve one another. And over the time we worked together we built lasting relationships (some that persist to this day) that helped us weather a challenging project.

DEVELOPING EMPATHY

Empathy is a defining characteristic of both great leaders and those who are committed to service. One recent study found that empathetic leaders have the greatest impact on profitability and productivity in an organization.[a] And in our own lives we almost all gravitate toward friends and colleagues who have the desire and capacity to understand us. Defined as "the ability to understand and share the feelings of others," empathy is central to service. But how do you cultivate it?

Here are a few questions you can ask yourself when interacting with others to make yourself more empathetic and other-centered:

- ***What circumstances are impacting this person right now?*** Author John Watson (pen name Ian Maclaren) once wrote, "Be kind, for everyone you meet is fighting a hard battle." He was right. Each person is at the center of their own story, in a web of pleasure and pain, success and defeat. Ask questions to fully understand the situation a person is in, so you can develop a picture of them in the proper context.

- ***How must they feel?*** Imagine how that person's various trials and triumphs play on their emotions and motivations. If appropriate, ask them directly or use simple statements like "That must be hard, tell me more" to help them open up and feel understood.

- ***How would I feel or react in a similar circumstance?*** Put yourself in their shoes. Don't simply imagine how they must feel. Imagine how YOU would feel. How would you react? What would be your fears and incentives? There is some risk in this. The other person may be very different than you and may think differently about their circumstance. But the act of imagining yourself in their shoes can at least help you feel closer to it and generate more potential insight to explore with them.

- ***What do they need right now that I might provide?*** As someone committed to serving others, think about ways you might be helpful to them. This may be as simple as listening—sometimes people just want to be heard and don't want your solutions. Or you may need to take a more active role in helping them to resolve their problems.

- ***How can I make this person feel heard and understood?*** Part of your developing empathy is communicating to the other person your caring and concern. When someone tells you something complicated in their life, paraphrase it back to them to show them you are listening. Ask thoughtful questions. And make comments that show you've not just heard them but understand and deeply feel the emotions their situation must cause.

Empathy can't and shouldn't be faked. It should be heartfelt. But for those not naturally empathetic, developing a habit of asking these questions can cultivate a greater proficiency with empathy over time.

a. Michael Schneider, "A Google Study Revealed That the Best Managers Use Emotional Intelligence and Share This One Trait," *Inc.*, November 16, 2017, https://www.inc.com/michael-schneider/a-google-study-revealed-that-best-managers-use-emotional-intelligence-share-this-1-trait.html.

We'll more fully investigate the importance of investing in positive relationships in the next chapter, but one of the easiest opportunities for service each of us has is in service to our work colleagues. Sometimes this service is formal—a manager dedicated to the development of her employees, a mentor dedicated to her mentee, an employee trying to make her boss successful. Sometimes it's informal or semiformal—pitching in when a colleague is ill, taking time out to encourage or coach someone, simply making an effort to chat with colleagues and know them personally. But whatever form it takes, it's critical. Tynesia Boyea-Robinson, founder of CapEQ and one of the most relational and other-centered people I know, articulates this well:

> *[I] love people and I love problem solving, and I tend to problem solve now for people. Like how do people live their best lives and be their best selves? . . . [T]he concept of talent is basically that people are valuable and worth something. And there's just way too many people whose lives are set up where that's not what they're told or what they feel every day—and it's just not true.*

A workplace in which colleagues serve one another is a happier, healthier, more productive one. And there's real purpose to helping people live as their best selves. To quote Emma Seppälä and Kim Cameron, who have written extensively on the subject, "When organizations develop positive, virtuous cultures they achieve significantly higher levels of organizational effectiveness—

including financial performance, customer satisfaction, productivity, and employee engagement."[4] When we serve our colleagues selflessly, we also experience greater purpose.

Community

You may remember our friend Rufus Massey, who built the Berry College Student Enterprises, from earlier in the book. Rufus worked through a variety of careers in his life but found higher education the most rewarding—particularly the opportunity to build student leaders. Rufus eventually ran the school's student work program, and he described to me how he'd help students find meaning even in jobs others might class as menial, like landscaping the school's 27,000-acre campus.

Berry's campus is consistently rated as one of the 10 most beautiful in the United States, and Rufus helped students see how their work mowing lawns and raking leaves wasn't only a service to one another—but to everyone who was inspired by the beauty of the place. Each and every one of them was contributing to the construction of this outdoor cathedral that could only exist by their mutual hard work and service to each other.

What communities are you a part of, and what are they trying to accomplish? At work, perhaps you're part of a customer service team dedicated to improving every interaction with clients and creating an environment in which you and your colleagues can serve with purpose. In your household, your service might be connecting with and supporting each member of your family in unique ways. Or it might be creating a close friend group in which each person feels supported by everyone else in both the peaks and valleys of life.

Thinking through the communities we belong to—neighborhoods, schools, businesses, organizations, families, friend groups, cities, countries, and everything in between—and how we can uniquely serve others in that community can be one of life's most fulfilling pursuits.

Capital

I previously worked for an asset management company where one of our teams had a wonderful painting behind the reception desk in their office. The piece showed firefighters, teachers, and police officers at work. It was a reminder to that group of the real purpose of their work. Many of their clients are large public pension plans responsible for the retirement and financial wellness of millions of public servants (often, for example, teachers, firefighters, and police officers). And while it would be easy for them to see their work—investing—as simply a numbers game, generating the greatest return at the lowest risk, the painting is a reminder that there are real people behind those pension plans and that their team is the fiduciary of these peoples' financial health.

"Shareholder" has become an almost derogatory term for many in business—some people have a picture of fat cats buying new yachts based on the performance of the companies they own. But it's important to remember that for most companies—particularly those that are publicly traded—the end shareholder is often a corporate retirement plan, public pension, 529 education savings plan, or other entity that is investing in that company to secure a dignified retirement, opportunity for higher education, or financial safety net for regular, hard-working individuals everywhere in the world. Are there some rich people investing? Sure. But of the roughly $98.5 trillion of investable assets in the world, approximately $30 trillion is in retirement plans for everyday people, $13.9 trillion is managed by insurance companies (for providing life insurance and health insurance, for example, to their participants), $3.7 trillion are in sovereign wealth funds (often dedicated to securing resources for citizens of a country), and $2.3 trillion are invested by nonprofit endowments and foundations. Even the $40.4 trillion in the market invested by individuals is often for the benefit of regular people like you and me.[5] The people behind these sources of capital are all hoping for a better future and trusting your company with those resources. Remembering exactly who most shareholders—providers of capital—are can make the responsibilities of people in any organization more fulfilling.

Who owns your company? Is it a partnership? A publicly traded corporation? Even if it's held by a private equity group, remember that almost all private equity capital comes from retirement plans, endowments, foundations, and other institutions. Look at your own 401(k) plan and see the variety of companies in which you are a shareholder. You may not be able to connect directly with the end beneficiaries of this shareholding, but you can certainly feel better about the work you are doing for them.

Partners

Umaimah Mendhro spent her early life as a Pakistani refugee, then moved to the United States where she became a successful corporate executive. She's developed nonprofits to build schools in the developing world. And most recently she's the founder and CEO of an innovative fashion company, Vida.

Vida sells beautiful clothing, handbags, and accessories. But its model, which the company's website refers to as "a global partnership of cocreators," truly sets it apart. Seeing the ways in which clothing companies in the developed world often took advantage of their designers and of their suppliers in the developing world, Umaimah built the company explicitly to serve not only consumers but her partners—designers and producers—as well. The company sources designs from diverse people around the world and pays above-market wages to its suppliers in places like Pakistan. Founded with two scarves and two tops, the company now "has 90+ products from over 125,000 artists in over 150 countries" and has collaborated with the likes of Cher and Frank Lloyd Wright.

An increasing number of companies like Vida are taking seriously their service to their partners—companies like Thrive Farmers coffee, a provider of fair-trade coffee, and Cotopaxi, the innovative and colorful outdoor sports and fitness brand founded by Davis Smith in Utah. But all of us have partners in our businesses—from consulting and accounting firms to cleaning services and computer providers. And each partner offers an opportunity to give back. We may not be able to fully transform our business model to serve these customers like Umaimah Mendhro has, but when we can't, we can offer a kind word, patience, and a spirit of partnership that can make the interaction more purposeful for both sides. This is relevant throughout an organization—from the facilities manager who works with an outsourced janitorial team to the procurement executive negotiating with providers all day. Editors work with authors, marketers, and visual artists, for example, and have an ability to impact all of those people as well as the readers for whom they are crafting great books and articles. Remembering that those who serve us as partners are individuals whom we can treat with dignity is an important part of effective and purposeful partnership.

People you love

Dr. Ben Carson's story is inspirational. He grew up desperately poor but went on to Yale and became one of the most well-regarded surgeons in the world, running pediatric neurosurgery at Johns Hopkins at 33 and accumulating a string of meaningful career accolades including becoming the United States Secretary of Health and Human Services after the completion of his medical career. But as Carson has often related, there would have been no Ben Carson without his indefatigable mother Sonya Carson.

Sonya was raised in foster homes and never learned to read, leaving school with a third-grade education. She married a 28-year-old man when she was 13 and ultimately left him when she found out he'd never divorced his previous wife. She raised Ben and his brother Curtis as a single mother and often worked two or three jobs to make ends meet for her small family, relying on her faith in God and the purpose she found in her boys to give her hope. I'm not privy to the jobs Ms. Carson worked, but I can imagine they were often unglamorous and difficult. But because she was so driven and dedicated, her son could rise to heights she herself could never imagine, saving the lives of thousands of children in his medical career. Her jobs were likely challenging, but they had enormous, world-changing purpose even when that purpose was hard to see.

Most of us don't have the luxury of working solely for fun. We may enjoy our jobs, but we also work to earn money to pay bills. Even at this basic level, though, work can become a meaningful act of service. Parents often work hard to invest in their children; those without kids often help support aging parents or other relatives. Others use their resources to support organizations they love in the community or their friends in times of need. It's rare to find someone working with only their personal needs in mind.

Who are you working for? Identify that person or group of people. When the hours are difficult or the tasks are unglamorous, remember that your work is an act of service for those you care about in your personal life. Keeping this front of mind will help you tie more purpose into your work, even when tackling the most tedious of tasks. It's a key part of the larger shift from thinking about what you do to who you serve—colleagues, partners, shareholders, clients, and community alike—and beginning to reconceive of almost everything we do in terms of service to others. If you're prone to forget why you work, put pictures or mementos on your desk that remind you of those individuals, so that even in the most difficult moments of the day, you will remember how much your work matters to someone you love.

Who Do You Serve?

Service looks different for everyone. But learning to focus in all things on giving back to clients and customers, colleagues, the community, sources of capital, business partners, and the people you love can make any life more meaningful.

Use table 9-2 to help you identify who you serve in each category. Beside each category, write down the names of one to three people or organizations you serve in each area. If you list organizations, write down specific

TABLE 9-2

The "Who do you serve?" worksheet

Category	Who do you serve?	How can you serve them better?
Clients or customers		
Colleagues		
Community		
Capital		
Partners		
People you love		

people within those organizations who are impacted by your service (with the exception, potentially, of "Capital" where a more general reflection may be sufficient).

If you have difficulty listing anyone next to any of the categories, use this opportunity to do a little research. Who is your organization partnering with? What groups do they serve? Who are you communicating with and connecting with through your work? Then, beside the names, draft a few thoughts on how you might serve them better.

There's no cut-and-dried answer for how to serve all of these different constituencies better. But once you've adapted your mindset to seek service in all your activities and for each group of people with whom you interact, the opportunities for advancing that service and improving upon it will become more obvious, and new opportunities will begin to arise. Think of yourself as someone committed to service, and gradually your actions will reflect that identity.

NOTES

1. "Giving, Rather Than Receiving, Leads to Lasting Happiness: Study," HuffPost Canada, December 20, 2018, https://www.huffingtonpost.ca/2018/12/20/giving-creates-happiness_a_23623679/.
2. "The Health Benefits of Volunteering," Corporation for National and Community Service, 2007, http://www.nationalservice.gov/pdf/07_0506_hbr.pdf.
3. Sylvia Ann Hewlett, "Good Works Can Lengthen Your Life Expectancy," hbr.org, February 12, 2009, https://hbr.org/2009/02/good-works-can-lengthen-your-l.
4. Emma Seppälä and Kim Cameron, "Proof That Positive Work Cultures Are More Productive," hbr.org, December 1, 2015, https://hbr.org/2015/12/proof-that-positive-work-cultures-are-more-productive.
5. McKinsey & Company Global Growth Cube, 2020.

CHAPTER 10

Invest in Positive Relationships

Thomas Rajan's earliest experiences were as an ethnic Indian from a Christian home, born and raised in the multicultural Islamic city-state of Dubai. Thomas's father was an oil engineer who moved to Dubai in 1972 immediately following the UAE's Declaration of Independence from the United Kingdom. Now a city of nearly three million, Dubai was a small town of under 300,000 when Thomas was born in 1981. As people rushed into the city to exploit the country's newfound petroleum wealth, the city became one of the more vibrant and pluralistic in the world. Thomas loved the diversity. "I remember growing up and going to school where I had people in my class from India and Pakistan and Australia and South Africa and England and the United States," he told me. "[A]nywhere you looked you saw this kind of vast expanse of humanity literally in one place."

Conversely, however, as Thomas grew older, he realized that the city was also rife with discrimination against people who looked like him. Upon graduating high school, he made his way to the United States. As his parents were not wealthy and had spent their savings on his two older sisters' educations, Thomas arrived in Glendale, Arizona, with $250 in his pocket, relying on his sister and her husband to help him make a life. Given his lack of resources, he enrolled at Glendale Community College and took out a loan of $1,754 dollars to pay for his first semester. He was scared he wouldn't be able to repay it. Then, two months after enrolling in the November of 1999, Thomas received a call that his father had died on the job in Dubai and he needed to return to his mother and move her to the United States. He was officially "the man of the house."

He dutifully picked up his mom and came back to Arizona. Not knowing what else to do but fascinated with airports from a young age, he took a job with America West Airlines as a customer service agent, and it was in that job that Thomas first discovered his two great professional loves: airlines and people.

Thomas fell head over heels for the airline industry, and he absolutely loved meeting hundreds of people every day, hearing their stories, helping them overcome their fears, and enabling their hopes and dreams through air travel. Twenty years later, he still remembers specific stories about the relationships, however brief, he made along the way.

Thomas recalled his first supervisor at British Airways, Anthony, who took him under his wing, and, in

Thomas's words, "He saw something in this 19-year-old kid and said, 'You know what? I'm going to trust you with responsibilities that usually people have been in the airline business for 20-something years get, let alone somebody who's 20 years old.'" Anthony, an Air Force veteran with a high school education, became Thomas's first mentor and was the first person he had write his recommendations to business schools years later. They remain friends to this day.

Thomas told me half a dozen stories like these. He remembers each one—particularly the stories of those who supported and sacrificed for him. And his love for people—his ability to create positive professional relationships at every turn and to authentically care for those he works with—shined through every example he shared. It's central to his purpose. It means all the more to him because he knows how much the help of others can lift a person up. That a young man from Dubai with such limited means could graduate from a four-year college with exactly $1,754 in debt—scholarships provided by others paid for the rest—and progress from customer service agent to an Ivy League business school to management consulting, running HR for the Boys and Girls Clubs of America (where he could invest in kids like him, connecting them to positive relationships), and back to the airline world, where he's now a vice president for global talent and total rewards at American Airlines. His story is one in which people invested in him with little reason to do so, and in which he's committed to investing in and serving other people, developing positive relationships with thousands of clients, friends, and colleagues along the way.

People are a big part of Thomas's purpose. He lives and breathes to learn from everyone he meets and to make each life he encounters a little better. Wouldn't you love to thrive like that at work? You can.

Fostering Positive Relationships at Work

There are few things as impactful to purpose as building positive relationships at work. In a prior chapter, we discussed the legendary Harvard Grant Study, which has, as its key finding, "Happiness is love. Full stop." And the broader psychological literature is crowded with findings about the importance of positive social interactions—including things like romantic relationships and friendship—to happiness and well-being. Martin Seligman included "positive relationships" as a core part of his PERMA model for happiness. Roy Baumeister and Mark Leary published comprehensive findings on the powerful need to belong in 1995. And, of course, human history has been littered with tales of the power of friendship for thousands of years—from Achilles and Patroclus to Harry Potter. The absence of such relationships can be deadly. Loneliness has been conclusively linked to intense stress responses, and one NIH study found, "Social relationships—both quantity and quality—affect mental health, health behavior, physical health, and mortality risk."[1]

These important relationships don't stop at the company parking lot. Professional relationships are critical to well-being, too. One study found, for example, that "employee satisfaction skyrockets nearly 50% when a worker develops a close relationship on the job."[2] That

TABLE 10-1

Investing in positive relationships

Method	**What it looks like**
Adopt a mindset of care and trust	Allowing people the benefit of the doubt and assuming good intentions; developing a greater capacity for empathy and an authentic care for the people with whom you interact; trusting people and giving them reason to trust you.
Be a mentor and a mentee	Signing up as a mentor in your organization or offering to be a friend or coach to a colleague who needs guidance or support; assuming the good will of others by asking for mentorship and then investing fully in the relationship with your mentor.
Focus on your most positive relationships	Consciously carving out time for professional and personal relationships that rejuvenate you; resisting the urge to spend all your time fixing broken relationships; and allowing yourself to enjoy your colleagues, family, and friends.
Repair broken or stagnant relationships	Changing your mindset about the person with whom you have a broken relationship and taking responsibility for changing your part of the dynamic; seeking to serve the other person and connect with them in a personal way to reestablish trust.
Continuously pursue new and diverse relationships	Actively seek out conversations and relationships with those different than you—in other departments, of different ages, with different skills, and of different nationalities, religions, and races; resisting the urge to stay comfortable and narrow in your personal and professional circles.
Make time for relationships outside of work	Keeping your work and life in balance and making sure to carve out quantity and quality time with spouses, children, parents, siblings, friends or others who matter to you away from work.

body of work shows that 30% of people have a "best friend" at work, and 56% of them were "engaged"; only 8% of those without a best friend at work were engaged. With data from Mental Health America showing "63% of employees experienced isolation because of a hostile work environment," the need for positive work relationships is pressing.[3]

Obviously, relationships in a professional environment will be different from those outside a professional environment—romantic relationships, for example, are fraught with complications in organizations. But positive relationships with good professional boundaries are not only possible at work, they are essential to developing greater purpose, meaning, happiness, growth and development, and well-being.

There are six key actions you can take to make your work relationships more fulfilling and meaningful.

Adopt a mindset of care and trust

At the heart of building positive professional relationships is caring about people. Mindset precedes practice, and the simple act of changing how we think about our colleagues can lay the foundation for improving our relationships with them in a way that is both inspiring and authentic.

What does this look like in practice? It may be as simple as showing small kindnesses to those with whom we work. Going to get coffee? Offer to grab a cup for someone else. Under tight deadlines as a team? Check in with a colleague who's struggling and offer to help. This may be particularly beneficial to junior colleagues or those whom others overlook. As Thomas Rajan says, paraphrasing author John Bunyan, "Every day try and find a way to do something for somebody who can never repay you."

As a leader, it also looks like investing in and trusting others. Very little is as impactful to a person's career as a senior leader who is willing to take a bet on younger colleagues and who invests in helping them thrive. Thomas's early mentor Anthony bet on him to run crew operations—a big job in an airport!—for their station when he was only 20. Now Thomas views his primary responsibility at work as, "creat[ing] and sustain[ing] an environment in which your team can thrive." And he constantly looks for opportunities to trust others before they are ready, to take bets on people and allow them to earn that trust.

Do you have a mindset of service at work? Once per day, find an opportunity to do a favor for someone who can never repay you. Are you focused on creating an environment where your colleagues can thrive, trusting and betting on colleagues before it's safe? Think through ways you could hand off responsibilities to others for their benefit.

Find a mentor—and be one, too

Mentorship is simultaneously one of the simplest opportunities for positive relationship and one of the most impactful. A study out of Olivet University, for example, found that 76% of people think mentors are important, but only 37% have one.[4] Mentorship for young people decreases depression and increases social acceptance and likelihood of college attendance.[5] And in a professional setting, people who are mentored experience higher compensation, more opportunity, and increased satisfaction.[6]

What can this look like for you? First, it's important to realize that mentorship is a two-way street. One thing

I've consistently noticed in my teams is that everyone wants a mentor, but most people are not serving as mentors themselves. Don't be selfish! It's important that you find a mentor, but at every stage of life, you can also *be* a mentor. If you're new to the workforce, invest in someone from your old college. If you're a junior manager in a company, don't become so wrapped up in your professional ambitions that you forget the critical importance of serving others. Find someone new to the organization and work with them. Adopt a simple rule: For every person whom you're asking to mentor you, choose one person you can mentor.

Then pursue these relationships formally and informally. Many organizations offer formal mentorship programs—75% of *Fortune* 500 companies by one count.[7] If your organization does, sign up both to be mentored and to mentor. If your organization does not, approach your manager or HR department to see if they would be comfortable attempting to structure one for your team. These formal work mentorship programs can be helpful to expanding your network within the company as well as thoughtfully navigating the organization around you.

Additionally, while it's important to have relationships within your organization, it's also important to have mentors who aren't directly responsible for your professional advancement—mentors outside of work. This can be as formal as a "personal board of directors" (as advocated by writers like Priscilla Claman and Bill George) or formally asking someone you trust to meet with you regularly. It can also be organic, simply meeting with someone you trust and admire (inside or outside work) to talk.

Finding the right mentors and mentees can be a challenging process. There's no one-size-fits-all solution, just as there is no one-size-fits-all career or life. But in general, don't let the perfect be the enemy of the good—pick a few great people in your network and approach them for guidance. Think through four or five people you admire in your sphere (as we did in the "Mining" section of this book) and approach them to see if they'd be willing to meet and offer advice. It can be that simple. The sidebar "Finding a Mentor" can help you find the right match and navigate the relationship.

Focus on your most positive relationships

Strengths-based leadership has become almost cliché in the business world. Based on the pioneering work of Donald Clifton, Barry Conchie, and Tim Rath, among others, the strengths-based approach to work effectively encourages people to realize that they can't be good at everything and they are more likely to excel by leaning into and developing their strengths than by struggling endlessly to compensate for their weaknesses. In this way, individuals can be truly distinctive at certain things while relying on others to support them where they are less able.

A similar framework is useful for relationships. Sometimes we get stuck focusing endlessly on relationships that aren't working rather than investing in and enjoying those that are. Researcher Robin Dunbar is a pioneer in understanding the number of relationships a person can

FINDING A MENTOR

Finding a mentor can feel like an awkward process. After all, we're not used to asking people to help us in our personal and professional lives. But mentorship is too important to neglect, and a thoughtful approach can yield great mentors for almost anyone.

To surface and solicit great mentors, consider the following:

- ***Think about the people in your sphere of influence whom you admire.*** At work and in your broader community, think of people whom you admire for their integrity, professionalism, sense of purpose, and career. Sit down and write a long list of everyone you'd love to have as a coach.
- ***Realistically assess whether they can be helpful in your professional journey.*** Some great people simply aren't the right mentors for you. Can they relate, in some way, to who you are and the career you are crafting? Will they have time to do it right? Can they influence your career directly? Not everyone has to fit every criteria (except for having the time and inclination to take you on), but they should fit some.
- ***Double-check your short list for diverse perspectives.*** If you are a man, find at least one mentor who is a woman. Find some mentors who come from a different race, ethnicity, and/or educational background. Find at least some mentors who are not in your direct management line.

Look outside your company. It's important to have a list of mentors with balance.

- ***Where it's natural, make someone a mentor in practice.*** If you work closely with some of the people on your list, you might not have to formally ask them to be a mentor. Just find opportunities to work with them, and let them know you'd really like their guidance and counsel. Often, they will be happy to carve out time as a coach.
- ***Where you have to, simply ask.*** If there's not a natural way to simply start working with them, approach the person, let them know you admire them, and ask if they might be willing to grab coffee or a phone call with you periodically to offer you advice.
- ***Express gratitude.*** Even the most generous people can grow weary of an exclusively one-way relationship. The easiest way to repay your mentor is to simply express an interest in their life and gratitude for their help. Caring about your mentor personally and being thankful for their efforts will go a long way to prolonging the relationship.

Mentorship is critical to personal and professional growth, and mentor-mentee relationships can be deeply rewarding. Getting started with a mentor requires approaching the topic thoughtfully and reaching out boldly.

have. According to his work, most people are only capable of approximately 150 "casual" friends (a shocking number in the era of Facebook and LinkedIn). Of those, perhaps 50 are "close" friends—people you'd invite to a party. Fifteen are your close circle—people you could count on in an emergency. And only five are your close support group.[8] People shift in and out of these groups over time, but this is a reality check about the limits of friendship and the need to invest deeply in a few others.

This is true at work as well. You should be kind to everyone. You will interact with hundreds or thousands of people. But at work, as in life, you'll find your greatest happiness with only a few people. That's OK. If you're having a bad day, seek out your best friends at work. If you get good news, celebrate with them. Don't be so obsessed with either expanding your network or fixing broken relationships that you neglect those who matter most.

Repair broken or stagnant relationships

Hopefully, most of your relationships will be positive. But in any organization, some of your relationships will be broken—a colleague with whom your personality clashes, the person who was passed over for a job you received, the person with whom you had strong differences in opinion that turned personal, or merely someone with whom you've had conflict. Some of these relationships may never be great. But many will need to at least be neutral for the benefit of your career, your feelings of purpose, and the health of the organization. A chief financial officer can't simply avoid her treasurer, for example, and a manager would be foolish to have a stagnant relationship with a fellow department head. The key is to be thoughtful about which relationships need to be repaired and how we can repair them both through our own mindset shifts and through changing interactions with that person. This can happen in a few steps:

1. **Change your mindset.** One personal habit I've developed is a gratitude journal. Sometimes when I've experienced a challenging relationship with a colleague I'll force myself to think about and write down all the reasons I should be grateful for that colleague or their work. I'll also meditate on the good things I'd like to happen for that person. Both of these habits have the power, over time, of changing the way you think about a person.

2. **Serve them in some way.** As we've seen in prior chapters, service to others is in itself edifying and meaningful. In the case of a broken relationship it also has the benefit of showing the colleague with whom you've had conflict that you are personally dedicated to moving forward.

3. **Find common ground and a shared project or interest.** There's a reason colleagues will sometimes get out of the office to solidify relationships. Changing contexts—to a sporting event, a walk outside, a lunch table, or a pub—can help defrost otherwise chilly relationships and allow people to see one another as more than simple

colleagues. At work or away from work, finding a project to work on together or an extracurricular you both enjoy can similarly build a helpful bond.

Some relationships are not salvageable, and I would not suggest that you stay in personal or professional relationships that have become toxic or abusive in any way. But where a relationship that matters at work is simply broken, it's worth making a conscious effort at repair.

Continuously pursue new and diverse relationships

I grew up in a midsized town in the Southeastern United States, Columbus, Georgia, and never really had the means to travel. I went to college at a wonderful liberal arts school, during which time I had my first opportunity to travel and engage with a much broader set of people. But it really wasn't until I joined McKinsey & Company in a large city (Atlanta) a year after I graduated college that my world grew by bounds. I had the opportunity to travel to places I'd never imagined—Singapore, Egypt, and Saudi Arabia—and encountered a kaleidoscope of people and cultures. The relationships I formed along the way not only made me a better person (more open-minded and thoughtful) but they gave me incredible happiness and meaning. My story is not unique. You'll hear similar insights from people in Hyderabad, Kyoto, Shenzhen, Amman, and Scranton. The excitement of broadening one's world through diverse friendships and experiences can be an almost universal one.

There are huge benefits to developing relationships with people unlike us and to maintaining the constant wonder and excitement of expanding these new relationships over time. Diverse friendships can stimulate creativity, make you more open-minded, and reduce confirmation bias.[9] And, at work, diverse teams are better at gathering facts, assessing risks, and engaging in innovation.[10] No one should ever take a "check the box" approach to developing diverse relationships at work, but we should all ask ourselves if there are ways in which we can thoughtfully expand the diversity of our networks—racially, ethnically, by gender, by experience, by department, or by way of thinking. Doing so can help us to be more curious and purposeful about the work we do.

Make time for relationships outside of work

When the United States shut down due to the spread of Covid-19 in March 2020, I, like almost everyone, was confused and concerned. There was much to worry about—people getting sick and some dying, shortages of essential supplies, crashing markets, and skyrocketing unemployment. But in the midst of this chaos I found one remarkable bright spot.

At the time, I was married with three young children. Before the world went into quarantine, I would travel 70% of the time, often going into the office early and staying late. Working from home was a revelation. The time I saved not traveling (perhaps 10–15 hours per week) meant I could get through my work more quickly. And working from my home office meant little visitors who were not in school would pop in with regularity. We'd sneak out and go swimming in the middle of the day. We'd eat breakfast together. We'd have dinner together every night and read at bedtime. I missed my other relationships—friendships inside and outside work, for example, which aren't quite the same over Zoom. But my relationship with my little family blossomed, and I saw the remarkable impact me being home and present more had on my kids (particularly as our fourth child was born while writing this book).

Even before the pandemic I tried to make time for relationships outside work—my wife, my kids, my friends, my community. And I was reasonably effective. But like many people, I traveled and worked too much, and the pandemic threw into sharp relief the need for very conventional work-life balance in my life, including greater time with the people I hold dear.

Put real thought into your most important relationships outside of work. For most people, this will include a spouse or partner, close friends, parents, siblings, and/or children. In palliative care nurse Bronnie Ware's wonderful essay "Five Top Regrets of the Dying," published on the AARP website, three of the five regrets involve not investing more fully in relationships. If you've been neglecting these relationships—working too hard or becoming too isolated, for example—perhaps it's time to restructure your time to allow more for them. If some of them are broken, strained by differences or distance, perhaps it's time to swallow your pride and take the first step toward reconciliation. Almost nothing in your life will matter more.

Time to Invest

Perhaps nothing in life is as critical to happiness, fulfillment, and purpose as positive relationships. Countless academic studies, ancient texts, and pithy aphorisms testify across centuries to the ideas that friendship, love, and mutual care are at the core of what it means to be human. The return on investment from constructive relationships is infinite. If you've neglected this area for too long or, perhaps, even been the source of too much relational friction perhaps it's time to change your mindset and invest.

NOTES

1. Andrew Steptoe et al., "Loneliness and Neuroendocrine, Cardiovascular, and Inflammatory Stress Responses in Middle-Aged Men and Women," *Psychoneuroendocrinology* 29, no. 5 (2004): 593–611; and Debra Umberson and Jennifer Karas Montez, "Social Relationships and Health: A Flashpoint for Health Policy," *Journal of Health and Social Behavior* 52 (2010): S54–S66.
2. Jan West, "The Truth About Job Satisfaction and Friendships at Work," National Business Research Institute, https://www.nbrii.com/employee-survey-white-papers/the-truth-about-job-satisfaction-and-friendships-at-work/.
3. Michele Hellebuyck, "Positive Relationships in the Workplace," Mental Health America, https://mhanational.org/blog/positive-relationships-workplace.
4. Olivet Nazarene University, "Study Explores Professional Mentor-Mentee Relationships in 2019," https://online.olivet.edu/research-statistics-on-professional-mentors.
5. Youth Mentor, https://www.youthmentor.org/thestats.
6. Brandman University, "Exploring the Mutual Benefits of Mentoring in the Workplace," March 22, 2020, https://www.brandman.edu/news-and-events/blog/benefits-of-mentoring-in-the-workplace.
7. W. Brad Johnson, David G. Smith, and Jennifer Haythornthwaite, "Why Your Mentorship Program Isn't Working," hbr.org, July 17, 2020, https://hbr.org/2020/07/why-your-mentorship-program-isnt-working.
8. Maria Konnikova, "The Limits of Friendship," *New Yorker*, October 7, 2014, https://www.newyorker.com/science/maria-konnikova/social-media-affect-math-dunbar-number-friendships.

9. Miles Hewstone, "Crossing Divides: The Benefits of Having Friends Who Aren't 'Just Like Us,'" BBC News, April 22, 2018, https://www.bbc.com/news/uk-43784802.

10. Kourtney Whitehead, "Why Building Diverse Friendships Can Improve Your Career," *Forbes*, June 27, 2019, https://www.forbes.com/sites/kourtneywhitehead/2019/06/27/why-building-diverse-friendships-improves-your-career/#4f69896a6d21.

SECTION FOUR

Purpose in Your Organization

CHAPTER 11

Creating a Culture of Purpose

Shundrawn Thomas learned early on how good and bad leadership can influence peoples' lives. Growing up in modest circumstances on the Southside of Chicago, Shundrawn and his three siblings benefited from wonderful parents who taught them to live "other-centered." Both his mother and father worked, volunteered, carved out time for their children, and invested deeply in their church. But their material resources were limited, and Shundrawn recalls an experience his freshman year in high school—a tale of two teachers, so to speak—that taught him the critical importance of good leadership.

Shundrawn's English teacher was a disciplinarian who required all papers be typed and turned in precisely on time. Shundrawn's family could not afford a typewriter (and computers were not yet widely available), so he had to reserve a spot in the library to use one—challenging given that he was balancing a job and school even at that young age. For one paper, Shundrawn simply couldn't get a typewriter slot before the deadline so he handwrote the whole thing and visited his teacher in person to explain. She rejected the paper, saying there were no excuses and she would fail him. Shundrawn booked an after-hours slot at the library that night (Friday night) to type it, then made a two-and-a-half-hour round trip on the train to deliver it to her house. He got it done, but never forgot her lack of grace and the negative culture she created in her classroom.

By contrast, a math teacher at the same school noticed Shundrawn underperforming in class and eventually figured out (due to his constant squinting) that he was struggling because he could not see the board nor could he afford eyeglasses. The teacher sat him down and let him know she knew how smart he was and she wasn't going to let nearsightedness cause him to fail. She spent time to help Shundrawn find a nonprofit that would help him get eyeglasses . . . something he says moves him decades later. The environment she created in her classroom was one in which individuals felt seen and heard and were motivated to grow.

Today Shundrawn Thomas is one of the most influential executives in the world. President and CEO of Northern Trust Asset Management, which manages more than $1 trillion in client assets, the boy who struggled to afford eyeglasses and typewriters now leads more than a thousand people managing more than 1% of the invested wealth of the entire world. He's written four books, including his latest *Discover Joy in Work*. He's a frequent

TV commentator, the associate pastor of his church, and a stalwart of his Chicago community. And drawing from experiences like those two contrasting classrooms in his childhood, he's a firm believer that purpose, meaning, and joy should be at the center of organizational life.

Shundrawn sees mission and values at the heart of engagement. But most leaders fundamentally misunderstand organizations. In his words:

> *Organizations are inanimate things. They're truly made up of people. So, if you want people to be fully engaged, really committed . . . what you need is not simply their hands, but you need their head, their heart, and their hands. It takes a commitment usually to a shared mission and this thought of a compelling vision that they're looking towards.*

With this in mind, Shundrawn sees effectively crafting and maintaining an organizational mission as a process. First, he says you must engage with those within the organization to develop a sense of shared mission. It can't simply come from the top; it's got to, as much as possible, spring from the people in the organization itself. Second, in Shundrawn's words, "it has to intersect with what I call the personal mandate." In other words, it has to resonate deeply with a person's internal motivations in a way that helps them engage with it. And, finally, it has to be based on values. He notes, of course, that large, diverse groups of people have large, diverse sets of values but also points out that "when people come together in communities . . . you can identify values you share."

You can tell this matters deeply to Shundrawn. As we speak he is able to talk me through Northern Trust's mission, vision, and values without notes and says many other employees can do the same. In practice, this has looked like him regularly refreshing these topics with employees—surveying and focus-grouping them for their thoughts, engaging with them at lunches and in town halls, and walking the talk—making tough decisions aligned with their mission and values and then stating and restating them publicly.

The Power of Purpose in Organizations

Most of this book has been about each of us, as individuals, mining and making our purpose—and learning to see the multiple sources of purpose in our lives and how they shift over time. But now we'll turn a lens to corporate purpose—what a culture of corporate purpose looks like and how to craft it.

For those of us who work in organizations, corporate purpose—the kind we hold in common—is extraordinarily important. Workplaces that have a deep sense of mission and values with which we can align are more engaging and joyful to work for. And for those who lead teams or organizations, the ability to articulate and act on a shared purpose can be unifying and energizing.

While much of what makes organizations tick is shaped by executive leadership, you don't need to be a CEO or top leader to imbue meaning and purpose into your company. Almost anyone can influence the culture of an organization—even if that influence starts with one's immediate team. And people who are individual

TABLE 11-1

Building corporate purpose

	What it means	What it looks like
Core purpose	Vision or mission—the corporate articulation of why a company exists and the impact it makes on the world; a company's reason for being or "true north."	"To help humanity thrive by enabling all teams to work together effortlessly." "To organize the world's information and make it universally accessible and useful." "To refresh the world . . . To inspire moments of optimism and happiness . . . To create value and make a difference."
Values	The way an organization commits to working—a statement of how a company does what it does and the principles it will consistently abide by.	"Adhere to the highest professional standards." "Improve our clients' performance significantly." "Create an unrivaled environment for exceptional people."
Satellite sources of purpose	The way purpose is actualized by an individual's day-to-day experience—separate from but aligned with core purpose.	Community service organizations within a company that organize colleagues to do good in the community; affinity groups for women or others that help historically underrepresented people feel connected and included; a volunteer mentoring program for junior colleagues.

contributors today may very well be the leaders of the future.

In this chapter, we'll build on what we've learned about our own personal sources of meaning and values to create organizations that better unify and amplify meaning for entire communities of people. The first step in that process is articulating a model by which organizations can surface and set out a shared purpose. We'll answer three central questions:

1. What is a company's core, central purpose and how does it manifest?

2. What additional sources of purpose can a company introduce into the day-to-day lives of employees?

3. How does the way a company act (its values) align with its core purpose?

A New Framework for Corporate Culture

Most organizations are now aware of the centrality of purpose to the effectiveness of their companies. Some organizations have long practiced putting purpose at the center of their missions, from Tesla ("To accelerate the world's transition to sustainable energy.") to the BBC ("To enrich people's lives with programmes and services that inform, educate, and entertain."). But credit for truly popularizing the importance of corporate purpose rests with Simon Sinek, whose book *Start with Why* ignited a passionate conversation about corporate purpose that echoes to this day. Sinek argues that most people—clients, colleagues, and others—are inspired not by what a company does or how it does it, but by why they do it. That "why" is effectively a company's purpose and fits neatly in the center of how and what the company does—it is central to a positive corporate culture.

At some level this makes sense. People in a company want to know that their work is making a meaningful positive impact in the lives of others, and clients and customers prefer companies that seem to have their best interests in mind. Certainly the "how" and the "what" matter—Ford Motor Company's mission would have been toothless without its manufacturing process and great products. But it mattered that it also wanted to change the world by offerings cars to the masses and innovating more humane treatment for employees.

My only quibble with Sinek, in fact, is his assertion that an organization might have only one central "why." In truth, organizations, like individuals, are endowed with multiple sources of purpose—typically one central and deeply held mission embedded in a web of values and satellite sources of purpose that matter to individual employees. Figure 11-1 visualizes the basic components of purpose and values in an organization.

Let's explore each of these components more deeply.

FIGURE 11-1

A framework for corporate culture

Any organization must have a core mission or purpose—its reason for existing—and a set of cultural values that guide its behavior and the behavior of all colleagues. These values should resonate with the shared values of individual employees and lead the organization to create satellite opportunities for purpose and meaning aligned with its core mission.

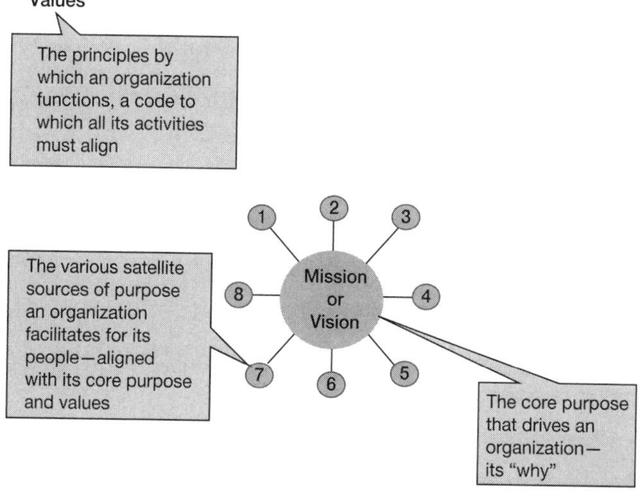
Values
The principles by which an organization functions, a code to which all its activities must align
1
2
3
8
Mission or Vision
4
7
6
5
The various satellite sources of purpose an organization facilitates for its people—aligned with its core purpose and values
The core purpose that drives an organization—its "why"

Core purpose—vision or mission

In some corners of management literature there are great debates about mission statements, vision statements, and the difference between the two. A rough consensus is that a mission statement describes an organization's core activities and purpose today, and a vision statement describes its aspirations for the future. We'll simply refer to these things as "mission" and summarily say that a mission should not only say what a company does but it should also imply or state explicitly why this is meaningful for the world. In short, a company's mission is its purpose, its reason for being, and its true north.

Why is this so necessary? I once heard UCSD professor Lera Boroditsky speak on the *Seminars on Long-Term Thinking* podcast about the Kuuk Thaayorre language spoken in the Pormpuraaw aboriginal community in Australia. The Kuuk Thaayorre language does not have relative spatial terms (for example, "left" or "right") only terms for absolute cardinal directions ("north," "south," etc.). English speakers can use the terms "north" and "south," but most often orient around themselves and use the terms "left" or "right." When you turn around, "left" turns with you—your sense of space depends on where you stand. If you are in a dark room and I ask you to point "south" you'll likely be lost. But if you ask a five-year-old child in Pormpurraw to point "east" she can do so instantly.

The Pormpuraawans orient around those points of reference fixed by sun, space, and earth. Consequently, their sense of direction becomes second nature. Everything in their lives is fixed by an understanding of its relationship to something else. Their artwork, their understanding of time, their place in the world. And that orientation means they're constantly aware of their surroundings, their direction, their path.

That's a pretty good metaphor for corporate purpose. Individual purpose can be changing, multifaceted, and entirely individual, as much of this book has argued. Corporate purpose, meanwhile, must be something like a cardinal direction that can orient an entire community of people and point them in the same direction. It doesn't depend on the individual (though it manifests through the individual), and it doesn't change when we change. It's something immovable—around which we must orient ourselves.

Does your company have a clear mission or purpose? What could it look like? A few of my favorites are:

1. **Movement Mortgage:** "We exist to love and value people by leading a Movement of Change in our industry, corporate culture, and communities"

2. **Google:** "To organize the world's information and make it universally accessible and useful"

3. **Walmart:** "We save people money so they can live better"

4. **Coca-Cola:** "To refresh the world . . . To inspire moments of optimism and happiness . . . To create value and make a difference"

5. **Genentech:** "To develop drugs to address significant unmet medical needs"

6. **Kickstarter:** "To help bring creative projects to life"

Some of these state their "why" explicitly (for example, Walmart's "We save people money so they can live better") and some do so more implicitly (Genentech assumes we see the good in meeting "unmet medical needs"). But each of these provides a succinct statement of what the company does and why that's meaningful.

What does your company do? Why is that meaningful? How can you state it in such a way that your organization's purpose is clear?

Values—the way an organization commits to working

Another primary source of meaning or purpose that most good organizations have are their values. This doesn't state what the company does so much as how it does it (for example, with character, integrity, a focus on clients, etc.). And often the "how" is as purposeful for clients and members of an organization as the "what" and "why."

My first exposure to company values was at McKinsey & Company. When I was at the firm, it had three core values:[1]

1. Adhere to the highest professional standards
    - put client interests ahead of the firm's
    - maintain high standards and conditions for client service
    - observe high ethical standards
    - preserve client confidences

- maintain an independent perspective
- manage client and firm resources cost-effectively

2. Improve our clients' performance significantly
    - follow the top-management approach
    - pursue holistic impact
    - use our global network to deliver the best of the firm to all clients
    - bring innovations in management practice to clients
    - build client capabilities to sustain improvement
    - build enduring relationships based on trust
3. Create an unrivaled environment for exceptional people
    - be nonhierarchical and inclusive
    - sustain a caring meritocracy
    - develop one another through apprenticeship and mentoring
    - uphold the obligations to engage and dissent
    - embrace diverse perspectives with curiosity and respect
    - govern ourselves as a "one firm" partnership

At McKinsey, these values align with the firm's purpose ("To help create positive, enduring change in the world") and its mission ("To help our clients make distinctive, lasting, and substantial improvements in their performance and to build a great firm that attracts, develops, excites, and retains exceptional people"). Over time, some leaders within McKinsey have failed to live up to this purpose and mission and to these values, including those who recently served large drug manufacturers who accelerated the opioid crisis in the United States.[2] But it is inevitably to these core values that the partners of the firm will return to try to correct the organization's errors. It's through a clear articulation of core values that organizations like McKinsey can hold leaders to a higher standard and reorient the organization after a public failure.

Think about the above. Who doesn't want to work at a firm with high integrity and a commitment to principle? Who wouldn't be motivated by an environment that considers them "exceptional people" and has an explicit commitment to creating for them an "unrivaled environment"? Whose purpose is not enhanced by a commitment to "deliver the best of the firm to all clients"? As we've discussed, service is central to almost everyone's purpose as would be, I'd argue, ethical behavior and self-improvement. And articulating values in this way can enliven and broaden the sense of meaning an organization can offer its members and other stakeholders.

When speaking of these concepts, I often hear the question, "But most firm's values are so similar. Are they really meaningful?" Yes. The most important part of a firm's values statement is not that it is entirely original, though tailoring as much as possible to the individual firm helps. It's that these values are authentic, that they are modeled within the firm and broadly held, that employees who demonstrate them are rewarded for them, that breaches are punished, and that all of the values are aligned with the company's core purpose.

What are your firm's—or even your team's—values? Even if they are not written down, inevitably you have them. Are they inspiring? Are they aligned with the company's purpose? Are they lived authentically every day?

Satellite sources of purpose—the way purpose is actualized by individuals' day-to-day experience

A practical reality of the modern organization (or any organization for that matter) is that there are multiple things companies do to encourage bonding, a sense of meaning, and the actualization of values that don't align neatly to that company's purpose. They are not misaligned with the core purpose of the organization, but they aren't tightly bound to it either.

These organizational initiatives take a number of forms. They might include company service projects in which employees go into their community together and volunteer building Habitat for Humanity housing or serving in soup kitchens. They may be company 5Ks that simultaneously allow for group bonding and fundraising for a cause. They may be mentorship programs in which company members provide guidance and counsel to underprivileged children in the community. They might

WHAT IF YOU'RE NOT IN LEADERSHIP?

The subject of corporate purpose and values can sometimes seem as if it's only for leaders—those who have the power to steer the organization as a whole. There's some validity to that. Organizational leaders are most obligated to assure that their firms have a clear mission, vision, and values which are authentic and adhered to. But there are many ways in which any individual can meaningfully contribute as well.

First, everyone in an organization should make a good faith effort to live for its mission, to strive for its vision, and to abide by its values. Only in each of us taking responsibility for doing so can an organization truly transform its culture to be more meaningful. That collective action is what gives the mission, vision, and value their power. And on an individual basis these will make your work and relationship more meaningful because they constitute the "why" of what you do.

Further, every individual bears some responsibility for improving adherence to these guiding stars. For example, my teams will often articulate our own vision and values—aligned with the broader organization but unique to the role we play and the way we want our

include company awards ceremonies where individuals who are particularly dedicated to the firm's purpose are recognized along with those who are good colleagues and friends. And they could include identity groups designed to support colleagues of a particular gender, sexual orientation, or racial identity.

team to function. Any team or individual can do that as a way of deepening and enriching the vision, mission, and values in the small group of people with whom you work day in and day out. On my teams, at least, I often ask a small group of team members—from individual contributors to managers—to take the lead on drafting these principles for discussion as a group. You could do the same.

Finally, try to positively influence the mission, vision, and values of the organization overall. The most obvious way is in the satellite sources of purpose in which you are involved. But if you notice your organization doesn't seem to have a purpose or values, perhaps you can find a way to speak up to your manager or to firm leadership in a town hall or other forum and offer (in a constructive way) to help the organization think through these things. There's some risk in that, of course, but there's risk to almost anything important. If done well, you could find that you've helped shift not only the meaning you feel at work but the meanings that dozens, hundreds, or thousands of others feel around you.

Few of these things relate specifically to a company's core purpose—though some can. A finance firm, for example, might target its community service toward financial literacy to more tightly align its volunteer work with its core identity. But such activities serve as meaningful, important "satellite" sources of purpose. They are the types of things a company facilitates that are aligned (or at least not misaligned) with its core purpose and values and help individuals achieve a more proximate sense of meaning and inclusion in their day-to-day work. They are important to the health of every organization, particularly as part of broader culture building.

Throughout this book we've explored how each individual has the opportunity to build his or her purpose, will have multiple sources of purpose, and will see those sources of purpose change over time. Satellite sources of purpose that companies build or facilitate for employees aid each employee in realizing his or her sources of meaning in more varied and practical ways.

What satellite sources of purpose does your organization facilitate? How do you tie them, if at all, to the firm's core purpose and values? And are there groups within your company for which you have not structured satellite sources of purpose who might not feel included? These opportunities should be found in the organization itself, and then leadership should empower individuals within the organization to construct them, breathing life into them as they do.

Aligning purpose and culture

Company culture is a competitive advantage. And at the core of a good company culture is purpose. Building a core purpose for your organization and then enmeshing it in a web of supportive values and satellite sources of purpose that can better enable people to craft those purposes into their individual work is the key to unleashing the "whys" of a great organization.

Before moving on, take a moment to answer a few questions to reflect on the purposes and value of the organization in which you currently work.

- What is the mission of your organization? If your organization has no mission statement, write your own based on what you see as the implicit purpose of the organization. Is that mission meaningful to you? How can you make it more meaningful, either as an individual contributor or organizational leader?
- What are your organization's values? If your organization has no values, write your own reflecting the culture. How do you live those values every day? How could they be improved?
- What satellite sources of purpose are you involved in at work? Is it enough, or should you consider joining a new purpose at work or even launching one? If launching one, sketch the idea here, and try to speak with someone at work about it in the next week.

Organizations without a mission, vision, or values will find a difficult time engaging employees, developing a positive culture, and fulfilling their purpose. Individuals in those organizations will find it hard to fully connect with the company and see its role in their lives and the world. Further, organizations that don't encourage employees to find their own unique sources of purpose at work are missing an opportunity to deepen their people's opportunities for flourishing and fulfillment in their occupation. A conscientious approach to these topics can help to create thriving individuals and an inspiring culture.

NOTES

1. McKinsey & Company, https://www.mckinsey.com/about-us/overview/our-purpose-mission-and-values#.

2. Gretchen Morgenson, "Consulting Giant McKinsey Allegedly Fed the Opioid Crisis. Now an Affiliate May Profit from Treating Addicts," NBC News, February 8, 2021, https://www.nbcnews.com/news/us-news/consulting-giant-mckinsey-allegedly-fed-opioid-crisis-now-affiliate-may-n1256969.

CHAPTER 12

Living into Corporate Purpose

Core corporate purpose, corporate values, and satellite sources of purpose constitute the "what" of corporate purpose. But what about the "how?" How can companies craft these three types of purpose thoughtfully, and once crafted, how can they facilitate greater alignment between the organizational sources of purpose they've identified and the individuals who make up their organizations?

One of the unique elements of Whole Foods's statement of its values is what it calls its Declaration of Interdependence. Presumably meant to mirror (linguistically, at least) the U.S. Declaration of Independence, written in 1776, the Declaration of Interdependence is meant to inspire images of a revolutionary new approach to what Whole Foods founder John Mackey has subsequently called "Conscious Capitalism." Whole Foods has a core purpose ("Our purpose is to nourish people and the planet") and a set of six core values.[1] Its Declaration of Interdependence however is meant to deepen, embolden, and enliven these things—offering them a kind of revolutionary flare. And the statement has been all the more impactful because it was drafted not by one man but by a series of people working together to take collective action. When it was first drafted in 1985, Mackey worked with 60 employees to come up with the statement. And it has subsequently been updated by broad working groups in 1988, 1992, 1997, and 2018. Over time, hundreds of people have contributed meaningfully to its evolution, and it remains a cornerstone of one of the world's most explicitly purpose-driven companies.

Why would Mackey go to so much trouble? He was the founder and CEO of Whole Foods. He had a strong personal orientation toward purpose and was successfully building a company with that orientation. He had the authority to draft something single-handedly and impose it upon those who worked for him.

But I suspect Mackey realized what a folly that would have been. In a document literally founded on interdependence—the mutual reliance and support needed between team members, customers, suppliers, the community, and the environment—it would have been foolish to draft the statement independently. And in working with such a broad pool of team members he came up with something that resonated throughout the company and was held broadly and authentically by those who worked there.

The "How" of Corporate Purpose

Most corporate mission statements ring hollow. And most employees are cynical about their companies' purposes. We saw this in the beginning of this book when we explored how most employees globally feel disengaged at

TABLE 12-1

Crafting corporate purpose

Method	What it looks like
Engage the organization comprehensively	Understanding the implicit mission and vision that exist in an organization and learning it deeply; launching an initiative to engage colleagues in crafting that mission and vision explicitly.
Periodically revisit your mission and values	Considering, every 5–10 years or around major transitions for the organization, an update to the mission, vision, and values that can keep them relevant and more connected to the current complexion of the organization.
Recognize those who live the company's purpose and values	Consciously seeking to highlight and reward those who go above and beyond to live the company's purpose and values—including highlighting people in town halls, creating awards for specific behaviors, and promoting and accelerating those who do.
Encourage both top-down and bottom-up approaches to purpose	Leadership teams must take ownership for the purpose, values, and activities of their organizations and should be the firm's key culture carriers, but they should also create an environment that encourages bottom-up feedback and engagement on these topics and a culture where leaders are receptive to ideas.
Be flexible	Holding an organization's purpose (but not values) loosely enough to adapt to situations as needed—just as Walmart did after Hurricane Katrina or as Cotapaxi did making masks during the Covid-19 pandemic.
Listen at all levels of the organization	For leaders in an organization, making the time to speak to a variety of stakeholders and encouraging authentic feedback and engagement.
Communicate consistently	A company's purpose will only be as powerful as its communication. Finding ways to launch the new purpose, to make it actionable, and to embed it in the organization over time will give it life.

work, unmotivated, and unmoved by the purposes their organizations purport to embrace. A recent Gallup poll found, for example, that "just 28% of employees strongly agree with the statement 'I know what my company stands for and what makes our brand(s) different from our competitors.'"[2] Only about a third of those surveyed said their company's mission and purpose made them feel their job was important. Why?

A big gap for most companies is not the "what" but the "how." Unlike Mackey, most leaders have not done the hard work of thoroughly engaging their people in the process of crafting a mission and values or in the launch and facilitation of satellite sources of purpose. As Shundrawn Thomas said in our time together:

> *Having a mission statement does not mean that people share in that mission. . . . So what you really need in a sense is a co-mission . . . actually engaging with people around the organization and thinking about not only how do you craft the mission, but how do you keep it alive over time and then fresh and compelling.*

There's no silver bullet to structuring this kind of engagement, but there are a few things any organization and any leader can do to more effectively make the crafting of their mission, values, and sources of purpose more authentic, inclusive, and broadly held.

Engage the organization comprehensively

When John Mackey started drafting the Declaration of Interdependence, he pulled in 60 Whole Foods team members to make the document better and more meaningful. Inevitably, this slowed the process. It likely led to places Mackey wouldn't have taken it alone and forced hard conversations throughout the process. But it resulted in something more authentic, inclusive, and widely embraced, making it worth the time and trouble.

For founders, this can be an easy process. Any founder starts a company with a mission, purpose, and values in mind but they can easily engage others as the company matures in the process of refining, reinventing, and restating these things. Like Mackey, a founder can bring everyone together while the organization is small and make the process of defining its purpose inclusive from day one. This can look like an off-site over several days at which the topic is discussed. In larger organizations, it could be achieved through a series of interviews and focus groups to get feedback from a large variety of employees.

Many leaders, however, are not founders and don't have a clean slate onto which they can write a purpose. These people have a more complex task. They walk into an organization with no clearly stated mission or values, or one where they exist but are not widely held. What are they to do?

First, they need to take the time to understand the explicit and implicit mission and values that already exist in the organization (whether they're written or not) by learning its history, understanding its people, hearing from customer and suppliers, and so on. Then they need to, like a founder, launch an explicit initiative to craft and create the mission and values that will define the company, much in the same way a founder would—leveraging large groups of employees, surveys, focus groups, off-sites, and other tools to make the process inclusive and definitive.

Regardless of the starting position, developing an inclusive process for articulating a company's core mission and values is critical to the success and authenticity of those statements.

Periodically revisit your mission and values

Why did Whole Foods update the Declaration of Interdependence in 1988, 1992, 1997, and 2018? Because inevitably companies change over time, the people in companies come and go, and the environments in which the businesses operate aren't static. There's a natural need to make sure that both a company's mission and values match the current moment and that the employees presently working at a company feel a meaningful attachment to its purpose.

Here, there is a delicate balance. I've seen organizations whiplash employees—revising mission and values with every change in leadership or in a desperate attempt to reenergize a failing culture. Companies that update their mission and values too often tend to find that doing so creates apathy and confusion among employees. If people think a purpose is only going to last until the next CEO or leadership off-site, they will be less committed to it.

But companies that never update their mission and values may find themselves out of step with the current era and misaligned with the team members who now constitute the bulk of their firm.

There's no science to the timing and nature of these updates, but they should be relatively infrequent (every 5–10 years at most) and should, where possible, be connected to some genuinely disruptive event—a large acquisition, entry into a new market, major changes in leadership, et cetera—that might justify a fundamental revisiting of an organization's core reasons for being. The process for revisiting values can be similar to the process of writing them in the first place except that most organizations will choose to build on their current mission and values rather than start from a blank slate.

Recognize those who live the company's purpose and values

A company's purpose and values are only as real as their commitment to incentivizing and honoring those who live them out daily. Chris Carneal founded his company Booster in 2002 to conduct "fun runs" and other events to "strengthen schools and students" by helping to raise money for students and teachers. Today, the company's overall mission reads in part, "Cultivating virtuous leaders who change the world . . ." and rests upon six "virtues" (Chris changed their "values" to "virtues" in 2019 to make them more aspirational and actionable)—gratitude, wisdom, care, courage, grit, and celebration. Chris and his team reinforce the importance of these virtues and their purpose daily by modeling their sixth virtue: celebration.

Chris tells me, "What gets celebrated gets reproduced, and we celebrate team members who are living out our virtues." This happens in myriad ways. Booster team members will organize dinners to acknowledge great achievements or gather in impromptu huddles to highlight these actions in the moment. Chris will post about team members on social media, and even, occasionally, write notes to their spouses about how great the person is and how much they are appreciated. These public encouragements are often accompanied by gifts—a gift card to a restaurant for a date night—and are always geared toward reminding people of the company's purpose and virtues and encouraging team members to truly live them each day.

How does your company celebrate people who live your purpose, mission, and values and correct those who do not? Do you approach the topic as intentionally as Booster, or do you allow too many of these examples to pass by unnoticed? Whether you are the CEO, in senior leadership, or simply heading up a small team, here are a few suggestions:

- Bake adherence to them into your formal performance reviews with meaningful consequences if they are not met. Accountability should be as clear as sales targets or functional performance.
- Award your culture-carriers and tell their stories—particularly where living the firm's purpose has required a meaningful sacrifice or trade-off.
- Be generous with praise when someone is caught in the act of living the company's purpose, and actively convene your colleagues in collective celebration of these moments—both in the moment and later in more substantive ways.

- Find ways to tell the firm's story aligned with those values and to celebrate historical moments in the firm's history when its purpose was most evident.

Without putting a firm's purpose, mission, and values into practice—without giving them teeth in the day-to-day lives of employees—these things risk becoming nothing more than words on a website, poster, or page.

Encourage both top-down and bottom-up approaches to purpose

One of the things we discussed at length in the last chapter was the concept of satellite sources of purpose—organizations and initiatives within a firm that help employees feel included and purposeful every day. Unlike a company's mission or values statement, however, these initiatives can change frequently and don't always have to be top-down or embraced widely at the firm level. Rather, they offer a way for the company to experiment, and as Shundrawn Thomas advises, to help meet people where they are with their individual sources of purpose and values.

In practice, these satellite sources of purpose are a mix of top-down and bottom-up initiatives. In 2020, for example, many firms decided at the leadership level to take a more active role in their firm's or community's response to the issues of health or racial justice through specific philanthropic and employee initiatives to help—from mask production to programs for more diverse hiring. They often weren't unilateral—many companies involved a broad set of employees in crafting and launching these initiatives. But they were company driven.

In other instances, these satellite sources of purpose are more bottom-up, powered by groups of passionate employees who are determined to make a difference in their own unique way, which are then embraced or facilitated by the organizations in which they take place. An organization might have local management councils, for example, that are responsible for leading that particular office's involvement in their city through community services and cultural events. It may have a women's group dedicated to celebrating female team members or generating greater inclusivity for women in the workplace. Or it may simply encourage every individual employee to think about ways in which the organization can be more mission- and purpose-driven and to periodically fund and support the best ideas. This combination of bottom-up and top-down initiatives not only uncovers better and more diverse ideas—it assures that those ideas resonate broadly with the people they are intended to serve.

Be flexible

Walmart has a very clear purpose: "to save people money so they can live better."[3] The company has done that by reinventing the logistics of retail, optimizing supply chains, building bigger and more efficient stores, and locating in less expensive locations around the world.

In the aftermath of Hurricane Katrina, however, Walmart's purpose shifted overnight. As documented in a brilliant case by professors Susan Rosegrant and Dutch Leonard, Walmart quickly became an extension of America's response to the storm and its aftermath when governments were overwhelmed. FEMA began using a Sam's Club (a Walmart affiliate) parking lot as a helicopter landing pad. Walmart stores in the center of the devastation began offering all of their merchandise—from hatchets to fishing boats to food—to first responders to aid in the rescue and stabilization efforts. When a local hospital ran into a drug shortage, a Walmart manager broke into their pharmacy and provided for officials. When federal supply chains broke down to the worst-hit areas, Walmart's world-class logistics organization stepped in, ultimately moving nearly 2,500 truckloads of emergency merchandise to areas devastated by the storm. Walmart was trading information and working together with FEMA, DHS, and local authorities. The "low-cost leader" was suddenly one of the world's most effective disaster response organizations, a purpose it had never previously imagined.

We've seen organizations similarly transformed in other crises. Waffle House famously played a role similar to Walmart in the Gulf Coast post-Katrina. Countless organizations like Adidas, Vida, and Cotopaxi stepped up to provide masks in response to Covid-19, repurposing manufacturing lines from one purpose to another overnight.

Did these organizations change their core missions? No. Were these activities misaligned with the core mission and values of the organization? No. But they were called for given the specific circumstances the companies and their communities faced at the time. Organizations and their leaders should always be open to flexibly expanding their mission, vision, and values—even temporarily—as the circumstances dictate even if that flexibility is not intended to result in permanent change.

Listen at all levels of the organization

Finally, companies and leaders need to make a simple commitment to listen. Shundrawn Thomas noted that since he's risen to his CEO role at Northern Trust Asset Management, he regularly makes time to walk the halls of the organization and to have lunches with his colleagues to hear what's on their minds. This can happen at all levels of an organization, from middle managers making themselves more accessible to their direct reports to team happy hours to town halls. Almost any organization would benefit from a firm commitment by its leadership to hear from employees and to take their thoughts, concerns, and suggestions seriously. This doesn't imply an obligation to act on everything—most companies are not and cannot function as democracies. But it does require an openness at all levels to hearing one another and the humility to realize that mission and values exist most fully in the hearts of the individual people within an organization. This can manifest in a few ways, both formal and informal:

1. **Company surveys:** Almost every organization should have regular "company health" surveys to keep a pulse on how team members are feeling and to make sure the organization's purpose and values are being lived. These should happen both

at the launch of a new initiative and regularly over time.

2. **Focus groups:** Particularly if you are in the process of updating or reshaping corporate purpose, engaging employees directly through focus groups to probe the organization's values, vision, and mission can be essential to surfacing and testing great ideas.

3. **Formal town halls and listening sessions:** Every organization and team should help give people a voice, and town halls and "listening tours" by executives can surface great feedback about the company on a consistent basis that leadership might not otherwise hear.

4. **Informal engagement:** Every leader—whether of a team, a business, or an organization—should devote real effort to spending time with and connecting with his or her colleagues. Eat in the company cafeteria and sit with new people. Ride the elevator. Walk the halls. Initiate conversations in each of these environments so people know you care and feel empowered to speak up.

Few skills are as critical to leadership as listening. And leaders who want to enable their teams to craft purpose should first take the time to hear from them. For more on how to engage your employees, see the sidebar "A Guide for Getting Started on Culture Building."

A GUIDE FOR GETTING STARTED ON CULTURE BUILDING

Leaders who want dynamic cultures must continually engage in the process of centering the organization and its people around meaning. Doing so will help the organization excel while encouraging fulfillment and engagement in the people the organization serves.

But being in touch with many employees can be overwhelming, especially if you're part of a large organization. Here's how you can get started. Ask yourself:

1. What three to five things can you do this year to better engage your colleagues in mission, vision, and values? Consider town halls, internal branding campaigns, company swag celebrating these milestones (like T-shirts, coffee mugs, or notebooks), or fun company outings to reinforce their importance.
2. What are two things you can do this year to help you more regularly listen to colleagues and

Communicate consistently

You can have an incredibly powerful conception of organizational purpose but that purpose will be toothless without good communication. Obviously, this process will look different depending on the particulars of the group in which you work. The CEO of GE may need refine your understanding of the organization's purpose and how people live it? Think of larger-scale actions, like a town hall or a focus group.

3. How can you make a difference by listening this week? Consider options that involve a few people, like taking employees to lunch, as well as one-on-one meetings.
4. Who on your team is living purpose well today? How can you highlight, reward, and encourage them? This can be as easy as sending an all-staff email highlighting their achievements or creating a monthly award to officially recognize those who carry the culture.

These actions don't constitute the entirety of culture building but can be a nice catalyst for those looking to get started on making their vision, mission, and values more memorable and meaningful.

an army of HR, advertising, and marketing executives to push the mission, vision, and values to its hundreds of thousands of employees. The managing partner of a small law firm may rely on townhalls, employee awards, and postings to the company's website or physical office. But a few elements will be consistent:

1. **Keep it simple:** If the vision, mission, and values are too complicated no one will remember them. Ideally, they will fit on a single piece of paper and be so clear the average person could memorize them with a few days' effort.

2. **Make it actionable:** Introduce employee awards for people who live the company's purpose or offer ways in which employees can recognize one another for doing so. At town halls, give people real-life examples from their colleagues of what it means to put the purpose into action.

3. **Brand the change:** Brand the new purpose initiative in an authentic way—perhaps putting it on T-shirts for colleagues to wear, issuing laminated wallet-sized cards, or changing the wallpaper on computers to create the sense that something has changed. But also take the time to elaborate on these concepts with colleagues so that they understand them fully and how they resonate with the deep culture of the firm. The slogans are helpful reminders but only authentic if they are understood and held close.

4. **Keep it front of mind:** Make sure the rollout is not a one-time thing. Each leader should seek to live the company's purpose and to encourage others to do so. It should find its way into company reviews and client presentations so that it's front of mind for people even as time draws on.

A few simple steps like these can assure that purpose with proper communication sticks.

A Call to Corporate Purpose

There is arguably nothing as important to a company's success as its corporate purpose and culture. They constitute an organization's most defensible competitive advantage (as highlighted in the book *Beyond Performance* by Scott Keller and Colin Price). More importantly, however, corporate purpose is deeply connected to the ability of individuals to achieve greater meaning and engagement in the organizations in which they work. And for leaders who care about the well-being of their employees, and individuals who want to thrive at work, there is little more important than that.

NOTES

1. Whole Foods Market, https://www.wholefoodsmarket.com/mission-values/core-values.
2. Nate Dvorak and Bryan Ott, "A Company's Purpose Has to Be a Lot More Than Words," Gallup, July 28, 2025, https://www.gallup.com/workplace/236573/company-purpose-lot-words.aspx.
3. See https://cdn.corporate.walmart.com/33/df/a80e56564 1f5ad6b1c2437fc4129/walmart-key-messages.pdf.

Conclusion: A Call to Action

How will you craft your purpose?

Over the course of this book, we've deeply explored the topic of personal and professional purpose, and we confronted three prominent myths: that purpose is something you find, that it's a single thing, and that it is static over time. We now know that purpose is mined from every part of our life and made when we consciously seek to craft it into everything we do. We can find multiple sources of meaning in our lives and embrace changes over time.

Your observations and reflections throughout this book (done in concert with a team of supporters and fans) should offer you insight into a life more consciously purposeful. You can reconceive your work and reshape it—through job crafting and craft mastery—to change the way you engage with your job and to connect it to service. But you can also use this spirit of purpose more broadly to think about how you can help others live more meaningful lives, whether that's through your organization or community.

My goal in this book has been to encourage you to think differently about your life and its meaning, and to move from hoping for purpose to crafting it. By completing the exercises and activities throughout this book, you should now have a good collection of your reflections, a clearer conception of purpose, and a practical plan to craft more meaning at work, at home, and in your community.

In graduate school we were asked to read part of a beautiful Mary Oliver poem titled "The Summer Day," which concludes with the lines: "Tell me, what is it you plan to do/With your one wild and precious life?" Predictably, the youthful answers from my classmates and me were all hopeful, optimistic, idealistic—and meaningful.

We all start that way, don't we? We have that sense that our lives are, in fact, wild and precious and that we have a chance, as Steve Jobs once encouraged, to make a "dent in the universe."

Experience, though, has a way of making us doubtful or jaded. Our optimism encounters disappointment. Our idealism runs up against the hard realities of the world. Our hopefulness and vision get mired in the details of our jobs, our bills, and our responsibilities. In the grind of daily existence, we simply push purpose to the side, opting for more urgent and practical pursuits. Or we get lured into hoping for a hero's journey—some near-miraculous event orchestrated by a helpful universe to offer our lives meaning—that never comes.

But you can create your own hero's journey. You can make one big dent in the universe or a thousand little ones. No matter your current circumstance, you can craft greater meaning in your life—and making that effort will matter to you and everyone you encounter. You may be in the midst of a dark moment or a hopeful one. You may feel keenly connected to your life's meaning or a bit disconnected and lost. But wherever you sit on that spectrum, know that I and everyone else you know has sat somewhere near you at some point in life. And we have more personal power over our feelings and circumstances than it sometimes seems.

Wrestling with meaning and purpose is hard. It requires you to carve out real time for reflection—not an hour here and there, but big chunks of time to think deeply. It will require structuring your thoughts and engaging friends, colleagues, and mentors to help you think them through. It may even require you to let go of the things that hold you back.

But I truly believe the time, struggle, and frustration will be worth it. It has been for me and for millions of other people. It's worth doing not once, but continuously as you navigate the multitude and changing sources of meaning that course through your life. And it's more important than the tasks you're thinking of right now that you'd have to pause to create time to process your thoughts. You've begun that journey with your reflections reading this book. And as your life progresses, I hope you'll revisit and refresh them again and again.

The glorious (and sometimes frightening) truth is that you only have this one life. It is wild and precious and passes all too soon. But it matters, often more than you know. Your work matters. Your relationships matter. You matter. Your life has purpose whether you see it or not, and it has the capacity to change the world, in ways both big and small. Even in those moments when meaning is hard to see, it's there—ready for you to seek, seize, and create.

Will you? I genuinely hope so. And there's no day like today.

Index

References followed by an "f" refer to figures, those followed by a "t" refer to tables, those followed by "n" indicate source notes.

Index

About the Author

John Coleman is an executive with experience at McKinsey & Company, Bridgewater Associates, and Invesco. He's currently Managing Partner at Sovereign's Capital, a values-driven investment firm.

Coleman is the author or coauthor of two prior books, including *Passion & Purpose: Stories from the Best and Brightest Young Business Leaders* (with Daniel Gulati and W. Oliver Segovia). A frequent contributor to *Harvard Business Review*, his work has been featured in *Forbes*, the *Washington Post*, the *New York Times*, the *Financial Times*, and the *Los Angeles Times*, among other publications. He has addressed groups from Coca-Cola to Seoul National University and has a particular affinity for speaking with students.

Coleman is active in the community, particularly with organizations devoted to education. He's a graduate of Berry College, Harvard Business School, and the Harvard Kennedy School. He has been recognized as a Presidential Leadership Scholar and as a George Fellow and a Zuckerman Fellow at the Kennedy School, among other distinctions.

Coleman lives in Atlanta with his wife, Jackie, their four young children, and a menagerie of small animals, including a bearded dragon affectionately named "Bruce Willis." He's grateful that his family offers him such a beautiful balance of purpose and joy.

You can follow him on Twitter @johnwcoleman or contact him via his website at johnwilliamcoleman.com.

Notes

Notes

Notes

Notes

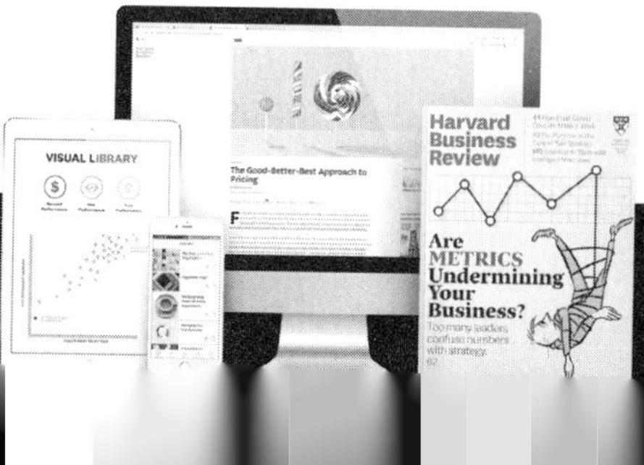

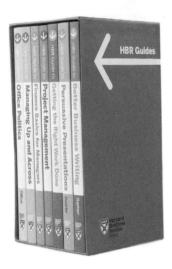